Cognitive Intelligence and Robotics

Series Editors

Amit Konar, Department of Electronics and Telecommunication Engineering, Jadavpur University, Kolkata, India

Witold Pedrycz, Department of Electrical and Computer Engineering, University of Alberta, Edmonton, AB, Canada

Cognitive Intelligence refers to the natural intelligence of humans and animals, it is considered that the brain performs intelligent activities. While establishing a hard boundary that distinguishes intelligent activities from others remains controversial, most common behaviors and activities of living organisms that cannot be fully synthesized using artificial means are regarded as intelligent. Thus the acts of sensing and perception, understanding the environment, and voluntary control of muscles, which can be performed by lower-level mammals, are indeed intelligent. Besides the above, advanced mammals can perform more sophisticated cognitive tasks, including logical reasoning, learning, recognition, and complex planning and coordination, none of which can yet be realized artificially to the level of a baby, and thus are regarded as cognitively intelligent.

This book series covers two important aspects of brain science. First, it attempts to uncover the mystery behind the biological basis of cognition, with a special emphasis on the decoding of stimulated brain signals or images. Topics in this area include the neural basis of sensory perception, motor control, sensory-motor coordination, and understanding the biological basis of higher-level cognition, including memory, learning, reasoning, and complex planning. The second objective of the series is to publish consolidated research on brain-inspired models of learning, perception, memory, and coordination, including results that can be realized on robots, enabling them to mimic the cognitive activities performed by living creatures. These brain-inspired models of machine intelligence complement the behavioral counterparts studied in traditional artificial intelligence.

The series publishes textbooks, monographs, and contributed volumes.

More information about this series at http://www.springer.com/series/15488

Nandita Sengupta · Jaya Sil

Intrusion Detection

A Data Mining Approach

 Springer

Nandita Sengupta
Department of Information Technology
University College of Bahrain
Manama, Bahrain

Jaya Sil
Department of Computer Science
and Technology
Indian Institute of Engineering Science
and Technology (IIEST), Shibpur
Howrah, West Bengal, India

ISSN 2520-1956   ISSN 2520-1964 (electronic)
Cognitive Intelligence and Robotics
ISBN 978-981-15-2718-0   ISBN 978-981-15-2716-6 (eBook)
https://doi.org/10.1007/978-981-15-2716-6

This Springer imprint is published by the registered company Springer Nature Singapore Pte Ltd.
The registered company address is: 152 Beach Road, #21-01/04 Gateway East, Singapore 189721, Singapore

Preface

Data mining is an integrated process of data cleaning, data integration, data selection, data transformation, data extraction, pattern evaluation, and knowledge presentation. The exponential growth of data opens up new challenges to extracting knowledge from large repositories consisting of vague, incomplete, and hidden information. Data mining research attracted many people working in different disciplines for quite a long period of time. However, the methods lack a comprehensive and systematic approach to tackle several problems in data mining techniques, which are interrelated.

The phrase *intrusion detection* refers to the detection of traffic anomaly in computer networks/systems with an aim to secure data resources from possible attacks. Several approaches to intrusion detection mechanisms are available in the literature. Most of these techniques utilize principles of machine learning/pattern recognition. Unfortunately, the existing techniques fail to incrementally learn network behavior. The book fills this void. It examines the scope of reinforcement learning and rough sets in handling the intrusion detection problem.

The book is primarily meant for graduate students of electrical, electronics, computer science and technology. It is equally useful to doctoral students pursuing their research on intrusion detection and practitioners interested in network security and administration.

The book includes five chapters. Starting from the foundations of the subject, it gradually explores more sophisticated techniques on intrusion detection, including Fuzzy Sets, Genetic Algorithm, Rough Sets, and Hierarchical Reinforcement Learning. The book serves a wide range of applications, covering general computer security to server, network and cloud security.

Chapter 1 provides an overview of intrusion detection. Two distinct types of Intrusion Detection Systems have been examined. They are referred to as misuse detection and anomaly detection systems. Next, the chapter outlines the types of possible attacks. It then emphasizes the main steps usually undertaken in an Intrusion Detection System. The steps include data preprocessing, discretization, dimensionality reduction, and classification. The data preprocessing includes data cleaning, such as missing value prediction, filtering of noisy data, and management of inconsistent data. Subsequent major steps in data preprocessing are data integration, data transformation, and data reduction. Data reduction has been examined in two ways: attribute reduction and object reduction. The next main step in intrusion detection is discretization, i.e., the transformation of continuous data into quantized intervals. The discretization techniques covered are equal width and equal frequency discretization, bottom-up margin, ChiMerge, entropy-based, and nonparameterized supervised discretization. The rest of Chap. 1 covers the classification of network traffic data. Finally, the chapter comes to an end with a list of concluding remarks.

Chapter 2 is concerned with the well-known discretization procedure of network traffic data. The discretization begins with preprocessing of NSL-KDD data set. Two specific discretization techniques have been examined. The former one, called cut generation method, focuses at the center of a data range dividing the range into two halves. The latter one deals with machine learning techniques.

Chapter 3 introduces the principles and techniques of data reduction. Data reduction refers to either dimension reduction or instance reduction. In this chapter, dimension reduction is achieved by two ways: Rough Sets and Fuzzy–Rough Sets. Instance reduction is performed using clustering algorithms. The rest of the chapter deals with experiments and reporting of results to demonstrate the relative performance of different techniques introduced therein. The metrics used include a confusion matrix.

Chapter 4 provides a novel approach to Q-learning induced classifier to classify the traffic data. In classical Q-learning, we develop a Q-table to store the Q-values at given state space. The Q-table is indexed by states as rows and actions by columns. After the Q-learning algorithm converges, the Q-table is used for the planning application, where the optimal action at a state is determined by the highest Q-value at the state. Here, the authors employ cuts of the continuous traffic attribute to represent the states, and the attributes represent the action set.

The Q-table contains immediate reward/penalty at a given cut for selecting an action (attribute). The Q-table adaptation is undertaken by classical Q-learning. To improve the performance of the Q-learning algorithm, we used rough sets to select a fewer alternatives from a long list so as to improve the classification accuracy. Thus, the attributes used in the Q-table are minimized. This chapter also aims at improving the speed of classification of intrusion traffic data using novel hierarchical learning. Here, the hierarchy is required to determine the attributes in coarse level at the higher level of the hierarchy and at a relatively finer level at lower level in the hierarchy. Generally, the reducts (important attributes obtained by the rough set algorithm) are used to represent the row indices of the Q-table. After an attribute at a given reduct is selected by Q-learning in a top hierarchy, the sub-tasks involved in the selected attribute are determined at the next level of the hierarchy. Thus, multiple levels of hierarchy are used to determine tasks as well as sub-tasks at higher speed of completion.

Chapter 5 concludes the book and provides future research path.

Manama, Bahrain   Nandita Sengupta
Howrah, India   Jaya Sil

List of Publication by the Authors Relevant to the Book

List of Publication by Dr. Nandita Sengupta Relevant to the Book

1. Nandita Sengupta, "Designing Encryption and IDS for Cloud Security", published in The second International Conference on Internet of Things, Data and Cloud Computing (ICC 2017) held in Cambridge city, Churchill College. University of Cambridge, UK. 22–23 March 2017 (http://icc-conference.org/index.php/conference-program).

2. Nandita Sengupta, "Designing of Intrusion Detection System using Efficient Classifier", Eighth International Conference on Communication networks (ICCN 2014), Elsevier, 25–27 July 2014, Bangalore, India. (http://www.elsevierst.com/ConferenceBookdetail.php?pid=80).

3. Nandita Sengupta, "Designing Intrusion Detection System and Hybrid Encryption for e-Government System of Bahrain", Middle East and North Africa Conference for Public Administration Research, Bahrain, 23–24 April 2014.

4. Nandita Sengupta, Jeffrey Holmes and Jaya Sil, "Detecting Intrusion and Designing of CCRX Dynamic Encryption Algorithm of a Network System", International Journal of Information Processing, 8(2), 37–46, 2014, ISSN: 0973-8215. Each of the IJIP articles are archived and indexed with prestigious academic indexes including Google Scholar, arXiv, getCITED.

5. Nandita Sengupta, Jaydeep Sen, Jaya Sil and Moumita Saha "Designing of On Line Intrusion Detection System Using Rough Set Theory and Q Learning Algorithm", Elsevier Journal, Neurocomputing, volume 111, pages 161–168, July 2013.

6. Rahul Mitra, Sahisnu Mazumder, Tuhin Sharma, Nandita Sengupta and Jaya Sil, "Dynamic Network Traffic Data Classification for Intrusion Detection using Genetic Algorithm", Springer, SEMCCO 2012, pp. 509–518, https://doi.org/10.1007/978-3-642-35380-2_60, Series Volume 7677, Print ISBN:

978-3-642-35379-6, Online ISBN: 978-3-642-35380-2, 20–22 December 2012, Bhubaneswar, India (http://link.springer.com/chapter/10.1007%2F978-3-642-35380-2_60).

7. Sahisnu Mazumder, Tuhin Sharma, Rahul Mitra, Nandita Sengupta and Jaya Sil, "Generation of Sufficient Cut Points to Discretize Network Traffic Data Sets", Springer, SEMCCO 2012, pp. 528–539, https://doi.org/10.1007/978-3-642-35380-2_62, Series Volume 7677, Print ISBN: 978-3-642-35379-6, Online ISBN: 978-3-642-35380-2, 20–22 December 2012, Bhubaneswar, India (http://link.springer.com/chapter/10.1007%2F978-3-642-35380-2_62).

8. Nandita Sengupta and Jaya Sil, "Comparison of Supervised Learning and Reinforcement Learning in Intrusion Domain", International Journal of Information Processing, 7(1), 51–56, 2013.

9. Nandita Sengupta, Amit Srivastava and Jaya Sil, "Reduction of data Size in Intrusion Domain using Modified Simulated Annealing Fuzzy Clustering Algorithm", Yogesh Chabba (Ed.): AIM 2012, pp. 97–102, Series Volume 296, https://doi.org/10.1007/978-3-642-35864-7_14, Print ISBN: 978-3-642-35863-0 2012, Online ISBN: 978-3-642-35864-7, Springer-Verlag Berlin Heidelberg 2012 (http://link.springer.com/chapter/10.1007%2F978-3-642-35864-7_14).

10. Moumita Saha, Jaya Sil and Nandita Sengupta, "Designing of an Efficient Classifier using Hierarchical Reinforcement Learning", ICGST Conference on Computer Science and Engineering, Dubai, UAE, 16–19 July, 2012 (http://www.icgst.com/paper.aspx?pid=P1121213150).

11. Nandita Sengupta and Jaya Sil, "Comparison of Different Rule Calculation Method for Rough Set Theory", International Journal of Information and Electronics Engineering, Vol. 2, No. 3, May 2012.

12. Nandita Sengupta and Jaya Sil, "Evaluation of Rough Set Theory Based Network Traffic Data Classifier Using Different Discretization Method", International Journal of Information and Electronics Engineering, Vol. 2, No. 3, May 2012.

13. Nandita Sengupta and Jaya Sil, "Comparison of Performance for Intrusion Detection System using Different Rules of Classification", ISBN 978-3-642-22785-1, ICIP 2011, Volume 157, pp. 87–92, https://doi.org/10.1007/978-3-642-22786-8_11, Print ISBN: 978-3-642-22785-1, Online ISBN: 978-3-642-22786-8, 5–7 August 2011, Springer Berlin Heidelberg, Bangalore, India (http://link.springer.com/chapter/10.1007/978-3-642-22786-8_11).

14. Nandita Sengupta and Jaya Sil, "Decision Making System for Network Traffic", KBIE 2011, 8–10 January 2011, Bahrain.

15. Nandita Sengupta and Jaya Sil, "Information Retrieval Techniques in Intrusion Detection", International Journal of Information Processing Volume 4, Number 4, 2010, pp. 1–6.

16. Nandita Sengupta and Jaya Sil, "Intelligent Control of Intrusion Detection System using Soft Computing Techniques", One Day-Control Engineering Symposium New Directions in Automatic Control: Theories and Applications, 26th April 2010, Bahrain.

17. Nandita Sengupta and Jaya Sil, "Dimension Reduction using Rough Set Theory for Intrusion Detection System" Proceedings of 4th National Conference INDIACom 2010, ISSN: 0973-7529, pp. 251–256, New Delhi, India.
18. Nandita Sengupta and Jaya Sil, "Network Intrusion Detection using RST, k means and Fuzzy c means Clustering", International Journal of Information Processing Volume 4, Number 2, 2010, pp. 8–14.
19. Nandita Sengupta and Jaya Sil, "An Integrated Approach to Information Retrieval using RST, FS and SOM" ICIS 2008, Bahrain, December 2008.

List of Publication by Prof. Jaya Sil Relevant to the Book

1. Asit Kumar Das, Jaya Sil, An efficient classifier design integrating rough set and set oriented database operations, Applied Soft Computing, vol. 11 pp. 2279–2285, 2011.
2. Santi P. Maity, Seba Maity, Jaya Sil and Claude Delpha, Optimized Spread spectrum watermarking for fading-like collusion attack with improved detection, Special Issue on Wireless Personal Communications Journal, Springer Verlag, vol. 69, no. 4, March, 2013.
3. Santi P. Maity, Seba Maity, Jaya Sil, Claude Delpha, Collusion resilient spread spectrum watermarking in M-band wavelets using GA-fuzzy Hybridization, The Journal of Systems and Software, Elsevier Science Direct, vol. 86, pp. 47–59, January, 2013.
4. Santanu Phadikar, Jaya Sil, Asit Kumar Das, Rice diseases classification using feature selection and rule generation techniques, Computers and Electronics in Agriculture, Elsevier Science Direct, pp. 76–85, vol. 90, January, 2013.
5. Nandita Sengupta, Jaydeep Sen, Jaya Sil and Moumita Saha, Designing of On Line Intrusion Detection System Using Rough Set Theory and Q Learning Algorithm, Elsevier Neurocomputing Journal, vol. 111, 161–168, July, 2013.
6. Indrajit De and Jaya Sil, No-reference image quality assessment using interval type 2 fuzzy sets, Applied Soft Computing 30 (2015) 441–453.
7. Nanda Dulal Jana and Jaya Sil, Levy distributed parameter control in differential evolution for numerical optimization, Springer Natural Computing (2015), pp. 1–14.
8. Pratyay Konar, Jaya Sil, Paramita Chattopadhyay, Knowledge extraction using data mining for multi-class fault diagnosis of induction motor, Elsevier Neurocomputing Journal, 166 (2015) 14–25.
9. Nanda Dulal Jana, Jaya Sil and Swagatam Das, Continuous fitness landscape analysis using a chaos-based random walk algorithm, Soft Computing, The Springer journal, pp. 1–28, 2016.
10. Nanda Dulal Jana and Jaya Sil, Interleaving of particle swarm optimization and differential evolution algorithm for global optimization, International Journal of Computers and Applications, Taylor and Francis, Volume 0, - Issue 0, pp-1-18, 2016.

11. Amit Paula, Jaya Sil, Chitrangada Das Mukhopadhyay, Gene selection for designing optimal fuzzy rule base classifier by estimating missing value, Applied Soft Computing, 55 (2017) 276–288.
12. Nanda Dulal Jana, Jaya Sil, Swagatam Das, Selection of Appropriate Algorithm for Protein Structure Minimization in AB off-Lattice Model using Fitness Landscape Analysis, *Information Sciences* (2017), https://doi.org/10.1016/j.ins.2017.01.020.
13. D. Dutta, P. Dutta and J. Sil, Simultaneous feature selection and clustering with mixed features by multi objective genctic algorithm, International Journal of Hybrid Intelligent Systems, 11 (2014) 41–54 41, https://doi.org/10.3233/his-130182 IOS Press.
14. D. Dutta, P. Dutta and J. Sil, Categorical Feature Reduction Using Multi Objective Genetic Algorithm in Cluster Analysis, Transactions on Computational Science XXI, Lecture Notes in Computer Science Volume, 8160, 2013, pp. 164–189.
15. Jaya Sil and Asit K Das, Variable Length Reduct Vs. Minimum Length Reduct - A Comparative study, Procedia Technology, Elsevier, 00 (2011) 1–10.
16. P. Dey, S. Dey, S. Datta and J. Sil, Dynamic Discreduction Using Rough Sets, Applied Soft Computing, Elsevier Science Direct, 11 (2011), 3887–3897.
17. Asit Das and Jaya Sil, An efficient classifier design integrating Rough Set and Dempster-Shafer Theory, Int. J. Artificial Intelligence and Soft Computing, Vol. 2, No. 3, 2010, 245–261.
18. Asit K. Das and Jaya Sil, Cluster Validation Method for Stable Cluster Formation, Canadian Journal on Artificial Intelligence, Machine Learning and Pattern Recognition, Vol. 1, No. 3, July 2010.
19. Amit Paul and Jaya Sil, Dimension Reduction of Gene Expression data Based on Rough Set Theory, Serial Publications IJCSIT, Vol. 1 no. 2 (2008), ISSN: 0974-8385.
20. Amit Paul, Anupam Ghosh and Jaya Sil, Dimension Reduction of Gene Expression data using Redundancy Removal Algorithm—Data Compression Approach, International Journal of Bioinformatics, Serial Publications, January-June (2008), vol 1, No. 1, 19–30.
21. N. D. Jana, J. Sil and S. Das, "Particle Swarm Optimization with Population Adaptation", IEEE Congress on Evolutionary Computation (CEC'14), Beijing, 2014.
22. Amit Paul and Jaya Sil, Dimension Reduction of Gene Expression Data for Designing Optimized Rule Base Classifier, Recent Advances in Information Technology (RAIT-2014), Springer, Dhanbad, India, 2014, 133–140.
23. Amit Paul and Jaya Sil, Feature Filtering of Amino acid sequences Using Rough Set Theory, International Conference on Computational Intelligence in Data Mining (ICCIDM-2014), Springer, Sambalpur, India, 2014 (accepted).
24. Zenefa Rahaman and Jaya Sil, DE Based Q-learning Algorithm to Improve Speed of Convergence In Large Search Space Applications, 2014 International Conference on Electronic Systems, Signal Processing and Computing Technologies, pp. 408–412, 2014.

25. Amit Paul and Jaya Sil, "Gene Selection for Classifying Patients using Fuzzy Importance Facto", IEEE International Conference on Fuzzy Systems (FUZZ-IEEE), IEEE, https://doi.org/10.1109/fuzz-ieee.2013.6622383, India, 2013, pp. 1–7.
26. Pratyay Konar, Moumita Saha, Dr. Jaya Sil, Dr. Paramita Chattopadhyay, Fault Diagnosis of Induction Motor Using CWT and Rough-Set Theory, 2013 IEEE Symposium on Computational Intelligence in Control and Automation (CICA), pp. 9–15, 2013.
27. Nanda Dulal Jana and Jaya Sil, "Particle Swarm Optimization with Levy Flight and Adaptive Polynomial Mutation in gbest Particle", In 2nd International Symposium on Intelligent Informatics (ISI'13) Mysore, August 2013.
28. Nanda Dulal Jana and Jaya Sil, "Particle Swarm Optimization with Exploratory Move", (PReMI'13), Proceedings. Springer 2013 Lecture Notes in Computer Science ISBN 978-3-642-45061-7, Kolkata, December 2013, pp. 614–621.
29. Nanda Dulal Jana and Jaya Sil, "Hybrid Particle Swarm Optimization Techniques for Protein Structure Prediction using 2D Off-lattice Model", In SEMCCO 2013, Tamilnadu, December 2013.
30. D. Dutta, P. Dutta and J. Sil Feature Weighted Clustering of Mixed Numeric and Categorical datasets by Hybrid Evolutionary Algorithm, 2013 IEEE INDICON to be held at Victor Menezes Convention Centre, Indian Institute of Technology (IIT) Bombay, Mumbai, India from 13–15 December, 2013.
31. D. Dutta, P. Dutta and J. Sil, Simultaneous continuous feature selection and K clustering by multi objective genetic algorithm, in: *Proceeding of 3rd IEEE International Advance Computing Conference* (2013), 937–942.
32. Monidipa Das and Jaya Sil, Query Selection using Fuzzy Measures to Diagnose Diseases, B. K. Kaushik and Vinu V. Das (Eds.): AIM 2013, LNCS pp. 19–30, 2013. © Communications in Computer and Information Science 2013.
33. D. Dutta, P. Dutta and J. Sil, Clustering by multi objective genetic algorithm, in: *Proceeding of 1st IEEE International Conference on Recent Advances in Information Technology* (2012), 548–553.
34. D. Dutta, P. Dutta and J. Sil, Clustering data set with categorical feature using multi objective genetic algorithm, in: *Proceeding of IEEE International Conference on Data Science and Engineering* (2012), 103–108.
35. D. Dutta, P. Dutta and J. Sil, Data clustering with mixed features by multi objective genetic algorithm, in: *Proceeding of 12th IEEE International Conference on Hybrid Intelligent Systems* (2012), 336–341.
36. D. Dutta, P. Dutta and J. Sil, Simultaneous feature selection and clustering for categorical features using multi objective genetic algorithm, in: *Proceeding of 12th IEEE International Conference on Hybrid Intelligent Systems* (2012), 191–196.
37. Nandita Sengupta, Amit Srivastava and Jaya Sil, Reduction of data Size in Intrusion Domain using Modified Simulated Annealing Fuzzy Clustering Algorithm, Yogesh Chabba (Ed.): AIM 2012, pp. 99–104, 2012 © Springer-Verlag Berlin Heidelberg 2012.

38. Moumita Saha and Jaya Sil, Dimensionality Reduction Using Genetic Algorithm And Fuzzy-Rough Concepts, 978-1-4673-0125-1 c_2011 IEEE, pp. 385–390, 2011.
39. Amit Paul and Jaya Sil, Missing Value Estimation in Microarray Data using Coregulation and Similarity of Genes, 978-1-4673-0125-1 c_2011 IEEE, pp. 709–714, 2011.
40. Tapas Si, N.D. Jana and Jaya Sil, Particle Swarm Optimization with Adaptive Polynomial Mutation, 978-1-4673-0125-1 c_2011 IEEE, pp. 143–147, 2011.
41. Amit Paul and Jaya Sil, Estimating Missing value in Microarray Gene Expression Data, FUZZ-IEEE 2011.
42. Nandita Sengupta and Jaya Sil, Information Retrieval Techniques in Intrusion Detection, ICIP-2010, pp. 447–455, 2010.
43. Nandita Sengupta and Dr. Jaya Sil, Network Intrusion Detection using RST, k-means and Fuzzy c means Clustering, Third International Conference on Information Processing, 2009 ICIP 2009 pp. 401–409, ISBN:978-93-80026-72-5, 2009.
44. Amit Paul and Jaya Sil, "Sample Selection of Microarray data using Rough-Fuzzy based Approach", World Congress on Nature and Biologically Inspired Computing (NABIC 2009), IEEE Computer Society Press, ISBN: 978-1-4244-5612-3 pp. 379–384, 2009.

Acknowledgements

We sincerely thank Shaikh Khaled M Al Khalifa, Founder member and Chairman of Board of Trustee, University College of Bahrain, for continuous support for research work by providing conducive environment, infrastructure, and facilities and for her passionate encouragement, and Prof. Shala Emara, President, Prof. Geoffrey Elliott, Vice President and colleagues of University College of Bahrain for their moral support. We are also sincerely thankful to Prof. Sekhar Mandal, Head of Computer Science and Technology Department, Indian Institute of Engineering Science and Technology (IIEST), Shibpur, India, for his support and providing infrastructure of IIEST. We are deeply indebted to Prof. Amit Konar, Department of Electronics and Telecommunication, Jadavpur University, India, for his valuable time and guidance for completion of this work.

Nandita Sengupta
Jaya Sil

Contents

1 Introduction 1
  1.1 Intrusion Detection Systems 3
    1.1.1 Types of IDS 3
    1.1.2 Types of Attacks 5
  1.2 Data Preprocessing 6
    1.2.1 Cleaning of Data 6
    1.2.2 Integration of Data 8
    1.2.3 Transformation of Data 8
    1.2.4 Data Reduction 8
  1.3 Discretization 11
    1.3.1 Classification of Discretization Methods 11
    1.3.2 Methods of Discretization 12
  1.4 Learning Classifier 14
    1.4.1 Dynamic Learning 14
    1.4.2 Dynamic Classification 15
  1.5 The Work 15
    1.5.1 Contributions 16
  1.6 Summary 18
  References 19

2 Discretization 27
  2.1 Preprocessing 27
  2.2 Cut Generation Method 28
    2.2.1 Algorithm for Generation of Cut 29
    2.2.2 Encoding Method of Center-Spread Technique 32
    2.2.3 Discrete Value Mapping 32
  2.3 Cut Generation Using Machine Learning Technique 34
    2.3.1 Optimized Equal Width Interval (OEWI) 34
    2.3.2 Split and Merge Interval (SMI) 37

2.4   Discussions on Results   39
2.5   Summary   40
References   44

3   **Data Reduction**   47
3.1   Dimension Reduction Using RST   48
       3.1.1   Preliminaries of RST   48
       3.1.2   Reduct Using Discernibility Matrix   51
       3.1.3   Reduct Using Attribute Dependency   55
3.2   Dimension Reduction Using Fuzzy–Rough Set   58
       3.2.1   Fuzzy–Rough Sets   58
       3.2.2   Rule-Base   60
       3.2.3   Fuzzy–Rough–GA   63
3.3   Instance Reduction   67
       3.3.1   Simulated Annealing-Based Clustering Algorithm   68
       3.3.2   Modified_SAFC Algorithm   69
       3.3.3   Most Significant Cluster   71
3.4   Results and Discussions   72
       3.4.1   Results of Dimension Reduction on Discrete Domain   72
       3.4.2   Confusion Matrix   75
       3.4.3   Results of Dimension Reduction on Continuous
                Domain   76
       3.4.4   Accuracy After Instance Reduction   77
3.5   Summary   79
References   79

4   **Q-Learning Classifier**   83
4.1   Q-Learning   83
       4.1.1   Extended-Q-Learning Algorithm for Optimized Cut
                Generation   85
4.2   Hierarchical-Q-Learning Approach   95
       4.2.1   Definition of Semi-Markov Decision Process (SMDP)   96
       4.2.2   Optimization of Linguistic Labels   96
4.3   Results and Comparisons   98
       4.3.1   Result of Extended-Q-Learning Algorithm   98
       4.3.2   Experiments Using Synthetic Data Set   101
       4.3.3   Results of the Proposed Hierarchical-Q-Learning
                Algorithm   104
4.4   Summary   106
References   109

5 Conclusions and Future Research 113
   5.1 Essence of the Proposed Methods 113
   5.2 Outstanding Issues 114
   5.3 Future Research Directions 116
   References 117

Annexure 119

References 129

Subject Index 131

About the Authors

Dr. Nandita Sengupta did her Bachelor of Engineering from Indian Institute of Engineering Science and Technology (IIEST), Shibpur, India (formerly known as Bengal Engineering College, Shibpur, Calcutta University). She completed her Post-Graduate Course of Management in Information Technology from IMT. She did M.Tech. (Information Technology) and subsequently obtained her Ph.D. in Engineering (Computer Science and Technology) from IIEST, Shibpur, India. She has 29 years of working experience out of which 11 years was in industry and 18 years in academics teaching various subjects of IT. Presently she is working as Associate Professor at University College of Bahrain, Bahrain. Her areas of interest are Analysis of Algorithm, Theory of Computation, Soft Computing Techniques, Network Computing. She achieved "Amity Best Young Faulty Award" on 9th International Business Horizon INBUSH 2007 by Amity International Business School, Noida in February 2007. She has around 35 publications in reputed conferences and journals.

Jaya Sil is associated with the Department of Computer Science and Technology in the Indian Institute of Engineering Science and Technology, Shibpur as a professor since 2003. She passed out B.E. in Electronics and Telecommunication Engineering from B.E. College under Calcutta University, India on 1984 and M.E. (Tele) from Jadavpur University, Kolkata, India on 1986. Professor Jaya Sil obtained her Ph.D. (Engineering) degree from Jadavpur University, Kolkata on 1996 in the topic Artificial Intelligence. She started her teaching career from B.E. College, Howrah, India in the department of Computer Science and Technology as a lecturer on 1987. Professor Sil worked as Postdoctoral Fellow in Nanyang Technological University, Singapore during 2002–2003. Professor Sil visited Bioinformatics Lab in Husar, Heidelberg, Germany for collaborative research. INSA Senior scientist fellowship has been awarded to her and she visited Wraclaw University of Technology, Poland in 2012. Professor Sil also delivered tutorial, invited talk, presenting papers and chairing sessions in different International conferences in abroad and India. Professor Sil has more than 200 research papers in the field of Bioinformatics, Machine learning and Image Processing along with applications in different Engineering fields. She has published many books and several book chapters and acted as reviewers in IEEE, Elsevier and Springer Journals.

Chapter 1
Introduction

Over the last two decades, information systems have revolutionized with more computer networking, Internets, World Wide Web (www), and Internet of Things (IoT). This resulted in a voluminous increase in both static and dynamic data size, offering a high chance of having potential threats to the global information infrastructure. From the statistics of reported vulnerabilities [1] by Computer Emergency Response Team (CERT) at Carnegie Mellon University (CMU), it is apparent that vulnerable reported attacks have increased exponentially during last few years. Cyber-attack is a widely used terminology to represent all possible attacks to computer systems. It includes computer virus, hacking, and password cracking to have access to the system. A lot many computer security techniques have been evolved in the last decade. A good security system offers the benefits of protecting important information of a company from possible attacks. The security policies of companies/organizations differ due to diversity in their missions. One basic constraint in designing security systems is to protect privacy, integrity, and availability of information resources. Protection of information systems/networks is usually done by restricting accesses to system resources by antivirus, firewall, message encryption/decryption or cryptography, secured network protocols, password protection mechanism, and many others. Because of the dynamic nature of data on computer networks/World Wide Web (www), the above mechanisms of protecting information from attacks are not enough. One natural follow-up of the above requirement is to discover knowledge from the network traffic data to provide protection of system and network resources from various possible attacks. The book aims at proposing diverse techniques of knowledge discovery in data (KDD) and data mining to classify the traffic into two basic classes: normal and anomaly. The objective of data mining in the present context is to extract specific knowledge containing valuation space of given attributes which is the antecedent to produce a target class.

An exhaustive search on data to match the valuation space of each antecedent variable for a given class is useful but time-costly and thus is not affordable. In this book, we propose an alternative technique to reduce search complexity by the adoption of Rough Sets. Here, we organize the data containing several attributes $A_1, A_2, A_3, \ldots, A_n$ and a class C. Thus, a database consisting of m data items has

© Springer Nature Singapore Pte Ltd. 2020
N. Sengupta and J. Sil, *Intrusion Detection*, Cognitive Intelligence and Robotics,
https://doi.org/10.1007/978-981-15-2716-6_1

effectively m rows and $n + 1$ columns. An exhaustive search to find the similarity among the data items for a given class with respect to each attribute requires time complexity of $O(nm^2)$. Here, $O(m^2)$ is required to match the data items on the same attribute, and n such comparisons are required for n attributes.

Rough Set is an important mathematical tool to autonomously determine the discriminating features of objects for different classes. The "*Reduct*" in Rough Sets provides the minimal set of attributes that jointly fix a class. Thus, finding *reducts* is an interesting task for classification problems. Rough Set generally is applied on discrete data sets. Thus, while utilizing Rough Sets in feature selection of classifiers, we need a discrete relation space of features. Although most of the real objects have discrete values of features, there are evidences too that in certain domain of problems, for example biology, the biomass of bacteria/protoplasms is a continuous variable and often is expressed as range rather than a single term value. This book opens up a new methodology to transform a continuous feature space into discrete form, so as to apply Rough Sets for feature selection in classification problems.

Rough Set provides a formal approach to determine the dissimilarities of features between each pair of objects. Suppose, for object pairs, $O1$ and $O2$, we have a set of three discriminating features: $\{v, w, x\}$. We represent this v or w or x (symbolically $v \lor w \lor x$). Similarly, for n pair of objects, we suppose, have n discriminating feature set for each pair of objects, given by $(v \lor w \lor y)$, $(v \lor w \lor x \lor y)$, …, $(w \lor y \lor z)$. We construct a discernibility function $f(s) = (v \lor w \lor y) \land (v \lor w \lor x \lor y) \land \ldots \land (w \lor y \lor z)$. This and condition $(\land)$ here represents joint occurrence of all the discriminating features, considering all pair of bytes. We then simplify discernibility function $f(s)$ by absorption law to reduce further. We next employ the expansion law to find out *reduct*, representing important attributes to determine the classes. Frequently appearing attributes are found out as a first step to obtain *reduct*.

Frequency count of attributes here is an important issue. Using more frequent attributes along with relatively less frequent attributes is expressed in conjunction form to describe the *reduct*. One important characteristic of the proposed work lies in discretization of continuous attributes. Although data loss is part of the discretization procedure, still its essence cannot be disregarded as discretized data only can be accessed by Rough Sets. One risk in discretization is the possibility of having inconsistent data, which may result in misclassification of data. This requires inconsistency handling as an important step for improving classification accuracy.

Potential attackers often find a way to infiltrate into a network. Development of an online Intrusion Detection System (IDS) that would classify system resources accurately is challenging. The classifier is to be designed with adapting capability which can modify itself with the change of environmental conditions to distinguish novel security attacks.

1.1 Intrusion Detection Systems

The term "intrusion" refers to the access of unauthorized user in terms of confidentiality, integrity, availability, and security of resources connected to the network. Confidentiality offers guarantee that resources should be available only to the authorized users. To maintain confidentiality, cryptographic techniques [2] are used for prevention of attacks. Integrity ensures that data should not be altered during transmission. Digital signatures [3] may be used as prevention technique against integrity. Development of such effective systems, which are able to detect intrusions with respect to time and accuracy, is known as intrusion detection systems [4, 5]. Intrusion Detection System (IDS) is designed to position within the computer system, which identifies the threats in data.

The key aspect of developing IDS rests on the hypothesis to exploit a system's susceptibilities based on the unusual use of the system [1]. All IDSs support this theory, in one way or another. Systems may use statistical approaches [6] and machine learning approaches, including neural networks [7], swarm intelligence techniques [8], Genetic Algorithms [9], and genetic programming [10].

Three fundamental steps are required to build an IDS:

(i)   Resources of data/information concerning the event records,
(ii) Occurrence of intrusion detection using analytic engine, and
(iii) Reactions are generated in response to the result of the previous step.

An IDS performs the following tasks, as shown in Fig. 1.1: (a) data collection, (b) data preprocessing, (c) intrusion recognition, and (d) performing corrective measures.

1.1.1 Types of IDS

IDSs are categorized depending on the host [11, 12], which may be single or multiple. IDS monitors a single computer as host by training the transactions of records in the operating system. The network-based [13] IDS is another category where IDSs monitor multiple computers or hosts connected to a network by imparting the related transactions and analyzing the movement of data across the network. Each module of an IDS, usually executed separately on each computer and reports is scheduled to a special type of module, called director, which runs on any machine. Other computers send information to the director, and so correlation of information is calculated in the director. The correlation is used to identify intrusions, which is not possible in case of host-based IDS.

Distributed Intrusion Detection System (DIDS) [14, 15], a typical distributed system contains multiple IDSs , working across various systems consisting of heterogeneous computers. Such IDSs are also called agents, interact among themselves, and maybe through a server, which performs centrally. The central server helps to monitor network activity in advance, analyzing the incidents which occurred in past

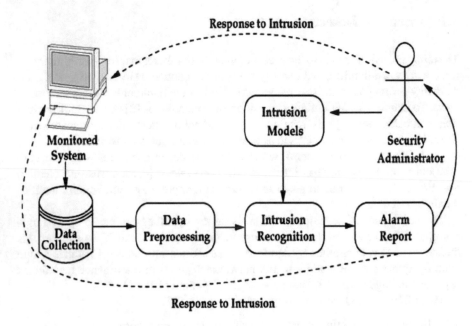

Fig. 1.1 Components of Intrusion Detection System

and sensing attack data instantly. Cooperative agents obtain a greater understanding about the activities of the network or agents communicate with each other, or with a central server that facilitates advanced network monitoring, incident analysis, and sensing instant attack data. With the help of the cooperative agents [16], incident analysts and security personnel get a broader view about the activities of the networks. A DIDS has the capability to manage the resources about analyzing incidents keeping its attack records centralized. The centralized records help the analyst to view the patterns comprehensively and predict the trend of future attack by identifying the threats usually occur across different segments of the network.

Based on the detection methods, IDSs are broadly classified as *misuse detection* and *anomaly detection*.

1.1.1.1   Detection of Misuse

Intrusions are identified by detecting misuse, which occur when predefined intrusion pattern does not match with the observed pattern. Therefore, intrusions are known a priori, easily and efficiently identified with minimum failure rate [17]. However, intrusions are evolved as a continuous process, and generally, polymorph; so, misuse detection method fails in case it encounters intrusions which are not known a priori. Regularly updating the knowledge base might be the solution but strenuous and expensive with respect to time.

1.1.1.2 Anomaly Detection

Anomaly detection model was proposed by Denningin in 1987 [2] who addressed the problem as orthogonal to misuse detection. Due to scarcity of abnormal behavior, the model is built considering normal behavior and identifies anomaly if the observed data deviate from the normal data. Two types of anomaly detection methods are there; static and dynamic. Static methods presume that the pattern of monitored targets remains same, for an instance, sequences of system call of an Apache service. In dynamic anomaly detection method, patterns are extracted depending on the behavioral habits of end users or based on the history of networks/hosts. Anomaly detection methods are capable of identifying unknown intrusions, but its limitation is to obtain knowledge about abnormal behavior because of insufficient samples representing abnormal behavior during training.

1.1.2 Types of Attacks

NSL-KDD data set [18] contains 22 types of attacks, used in the book for building the IDS and verifying the proposed algorithms. These attacks [19] are classified as: User to Root, Remote to Local, Denial of Service, and Probe.

- Denial of Service (DoS): In this attack, attempts have been made by the attackers to intercept the original users to availing any kind of service.
- Remote to Local (R2L): The aim of the attackers is to gaining access in the victim's machine without an account.
- User to Root (U2R): Attackers try to act as superuser by accessing the user's computer locally.
- Probe: Attackers should have the freedom to obtain important facts regarding the target host.

Most of the attacks belong to the category of denial of service (DoS). Some more types of attacks are encountered in the computer system, such as eavesdropping, snooping, interception, and distributed denial-of-service (DDoS) attacks, to name a few.

Eavesdropping— Eavesdropping is secretly listening the private conversations of others without their consent.

Snooping—Snooping is used to monitor activity of a computer or network device remotely.

Interception—It is one type of man-in-the-middle attack which intercepts the messages transmitted between two devices and alter those.

Distributed denial of service—Malicious attempt to disrupt normal traffic of a server or network. Target server and its surroundings are getting flooded by Internet traffic. As a result, normal users are not able to access the affected target and its surroundings.

1.2   Data Preprocessing

To perform data analysis accurately and efficiently, data preprocessing has a major role for better understanding of data. Preprocessing of data [20] plays a vital role to handle the data easily and suitably reduce complexity for subsequent analysis. Effort and involvement of time to obtain the processed input open new challenges to extract pattern or knowledge automatically from the data. A few tools and techniques [21] are available to preprocess the data, sampling [21], transformation [22], denoising [22], and more. In the step of sampling, from a large population, subset of samples is chosen. Data transformation is required for suitable representation of raw data, and denoising method removes noise from data.

Different methods for data preprocessing are listed below:

- Cleaning
- Integration
- Transformation
- Reduction.

1.2.1   Cleaning of Data

Incompleteness, inconsistency, and noise in association with real-world data are obvious. Missing value imputation, noise handling techniques, outlier removal, and dealing with inconsistency are the goals of data cleaning [23, 24] operations.

1.2.1.1   Missing Values

Different approaches to substitute/replace missing values to interpret data in a better way are available. Usually when class label is missing, the respective tuple is ignored. However, this method is not very effective, unless some attributes with missing values have been observed in the samples of a data set. Filling of missing value with manual effort is expensive w.r.t time and difficult if not impossible for a huge data set, with many missing values. The easiest method is to use a global constant, say "unknown" for missing values but it is not an acceptable solution. In case of missing value in different attributes, the mean of the corresponding attribute values is used to replace the same. The procedure is also applicable for the samples or objects having missing values and have the same class labels. Regression [25] is the widely used method for missing value estimation. Other methods are inference-based mechanisms considering Bayesian formalism [26] or induction method based on decision tree [27].

1.2.1.2 Noisy Data

Noise may be defined as a random fluctuation of a measured variable (signal) at discrete time points. Different techniques of smoothing to filter noise from signals are available [22]. Based on the neighboring values, sorted data are smoothed using binning methods [22]. In different bins or "buckets," sorted data are distributed, and smoothing operation on data is performed locally. When the data in a bin are replaced by the median value for smoothing, the method is named as bin medians method [22]. In another noise smoothing operation, i.e., bin boundaries method, first the minimum and maximum values of each bin are obtained. Then, the values are replaced by the boundary values which are close to the minimum and maximum values. Generally, the effect of smoothing is observed depending on the width of the bins, and more the difference, better is the smoothing effect. Equal width bins, with constant interval values, may also be considered as an alternative approach.

Regression method is used to smooth the data by employing a function for fitting the data. The best fit line is computed using linear regression method [25] considering two variables, one is called response, and another is known as predicted variable. When more than two variables are involved, we use multiple linear regression to fit the data into a multidimensional space.

Outliers [22] are also treated as noise in some applications and so removed from the original data sets. When similar patterns are clustered into a group and which do not belong to any cluster, they are treated as outliers.

1.2.1.3 Inconsistent Data

Our regular experience reveals that data of longer duration have high probability to contain inconsistency. For the same attribute values, class labels of objects change for various reasons and become the source of introducing inconsistency in the data set. Manual correction of data inconsistency is possible by employing external references. For instance, if error occurs during data entry operation, they are corrected by performing a paper trace. Additionally, possible inconsistency may appear in codes, which too need to be corrected by paper traces. Thus, elimination of inconsistency in codes along with data by paper trace method is time-consuming. Knowledge engineering tools [22] are applied for detecting violation of known data constraints [22], such as known functional dependencies [22] between the attributes can be applied to obtain the values which contradict the functional constraints. Inconsistencies may also appear during integration of data, in which case an attribute is represented in different databases with distinct names. Data transformation [22] is another source of generating inconsistent data, which is handled by different statistical and data mining tools [22].

1.2.2   Integration of Data

Integration of data [28] is an important phase of data analysis, referred to combining the data from number of sources and store coherently, like data warehousing. Sources may be more than one database, data cubes, or flat files. Data integration issue is not relevant in the present context and thus is not covered in this book.

1.2.3   Transformation of Data

Transformation of data [29] is essential in data mining operation for consolidating the data into appropriate forms. *Generalization* transforms low-level data into concepts at higher levels using grouping of concept hierarchically [22]. Using *normalization* operation, scaling of the attributes is done to keep the values within a range, specified earlier, and thus removes existing outliers. The data set often suffers from heterogeneity of data, which are standardized to maintain homogeneity among all the features by suitable conversion methods.

1.2.4   Data Reduction

Here, attribute and object reduction both are referred as data reduction, which are discussed in separate subsections. However, in the work, attribute reduction has been focused primarily.

1.2.4.1   Attribute Reduction

After the preparation of data, it is ready for processing based on the aims and objectives of the work. But in reality, the exponential growth of data makes it unmanageable even if very high performance computing environment and storage devices are available. Therefore, dimension reduction of data is needed for the improvement of computational efficiency at the cost of minimum loss of information. The goal of dimension reduction [30] is to select significant features by removing redundant and less important features. Dimension reduction helps in reduction of time requirement for performing induction. It also helps in making more comprehensive rules that increases classification or prediction accuracy [31]. Purpose of dimension reduction technique is to reduce amount of data while preserving the meaning of the original data. Dimension reduction procedure is applied by invoking proper discriminating measure for each attribute. Based on the measure, either the attribute is retained or discarded.

Broadly, dimension reduction has been categorized as transformation-based and selection-based methods.

Transformation-Based Methods These methods are applied when preserving semantic is not important for further processing of the data set. Two categories, namely linearity and nonlinearity techniques are discussed below.

Principal component analysis (PCA) [32] and multidimensional scaling (MDS) [33] are well-developed linear methods of dimensionality reduction techniques determining the structure of the data for obtaining internal relationships. Usually, these methods fail for higher-dimensional data. However, linear dimension reduction techniques are well-accepted methods on many applications.

Principal component analysis (PCA) is a common and popular dimensionality reduction technique with efficient computational algorithms. Features of a data set have been transformed to a set of new features using PCA method. The transformed features are uncorrelated, called principal components (PC). We choose the features which have maximum variants, and thus reducing dimension of the data set using linear discriminant analysis (LDA) method [34]. The ratio between class variance to within class variance in a data set has been maximized in order to achieve guaranteed well-separated data sets with different class labels [35]. The objective of the LDA method is to obtain maximum separation of the data sets that belong to different classes without transformation of data while PCA transforms the data. Projection pursuit (PP) [36, 37] optimizes the quality metric to obtain projected data set having lower dimension than the original one.

Nonlinear methods are applied as data set having nonlinear relationships. Nonlinearity has been handled effectively first using clustering algorithms, followed by applying PCA with respect to each cluster [38]. Greedy algorithms [39] are also applied within each cluster for optimizing the dimension of the data. Problems raised by these methods have motivated the development of techniques for handling nonlinearity with success. An extended form of multidimensional scaling (MDS) is Isomap [40] where embeddings are optimized for preserving distances among any two data points. The distance is called geodesic distances, calculated using shortest paths over enormous data sub-lattices [35]. Nonlinear degrees of freedom are measured using the MDS algorithm, representing low-dimensional geometry of the manifold. Locally, linear embedding (LLE) [41] method calculates eigen vector for solving nonlinear dimension reduction. LLE computes data embeddings to obtain low dimensionality in reconstructed data by preserving neighborhood phenomena, with high dimensionality.

Selection-Based Reduction The objective of selecting features is to obtain a subset of features, which is able to achieve high accuracy that could have been achieved before reducing feature set. There are two types of algorithms depending on the process of evaluation. The first one is *filter* approach [35], where an algorithm performs feature selection which is not dependent on learning. The *wrapper* approach [35] evaluates the feature selection algorithm along with the learning algorithm.

Rough Set theory [42–44] is used for feature selection, which needs a special mention here for its deployment in the book for reduction of information table. There is a minimum subset of conditional attributes called *reduct* (RED); therefore, RED $\subseteq C$ [45, 46] manifests the exact characteristics of the information system, as it would be done with the total conditional attribute set (say, C).

Rough Set concepts, *reduct* generation (derived from different computational intelligent techniques [35]), the equivalence (indiscernible) classes, *discernibility matrix* [47, 48], *attribute dependency*, etc., are explained in detail in Chap. 3.

1.2.4.2 Object Reduction

Clustering algorithms [49] are applied to analyze enormous volume of data by partitioning the data into number of classes, not known a priori. Basically, data clustering is a technique where logically similar information is grouped together. A distance metric is used to measure the similarity of data for clustering based on which the class of an unknown object is determined. Clustering is required to determine the class of an unknown data point. After clustering is undertaken, the clusterings formed contain group of system data points. Each cluster has a cluster center that represents the ideal member of the clustering. Clustering helps to identify the cluster of an unknown information based on its measure of distance with respect to cluster centers. If an unknown data point falls in a cluster based on the said metric, then this new data point is expected to have similar characteristics (features) with respect to all data points falling in the selected cluster. Different types of clusterings like hierarchical, partitional (k-means), and self-organizing are available in the literature [50–52]. Besides it, the current research explores hybridization of data set clustering as mentioned here.

In case, an object is categorized based on its belonging in a cluster or not and is referred as hard clustering [53], similar to determining whether an object is a member of a set or not. Soft clustering method [53] is applied when information about the objects is incomplete or features are vague. So, objects are not partitioned definitely rather belong to multiple clusters. For example, using Fuzzy clustering [54], the objects are classified into different clusters with varied membership values [55]. In many cases, where detection of boundary between different classes is crucial, Fuzzy clustering is useful to assign the objects based on their degree of membership values.

In traditional clustering algorithms, a data point is presumed to fall in one cluster only. Thus, the membership of a data point in one cluster is either zero or one, indicating its absence or presence in the cluster. Unfortunately, there exist situations when a data point ceases to be member of a cluster and appears in more than one cluster with partial membership function, such that sum of the memberships of the data point in all valid clusters $= 1$.

Several algorithms have been developed over the three decades to extend the traditional k-means clustering algorithms, which support hard clustering, indicating the existence of a point as a member/non-member of a cluster. One possible extension that needs a special mention is Fuzzy C-means clustering algorithm, which is based on the following primitives.

Fuzzy C-means [56, 57] clustering algorithm optimizes an objective function, to group the data points into different clusters, and other clustering algorithms are bit modification of it. Different optimization techniques like iterative minimization [58], Simulated Annealing [59], or Genetic Algorithms [60] are applied to solve vagueness using fuzzy clustering problems.

1.3 Discretization

Discretization [61] in statistics and machine learning is used to convert continuous variables into different distinct intervals, typically partitions into K equal lengths (intervals/width) or $K\%$ of the total data (equal frequencies).

Discretization is a process that performs using the following steps (i) sorting (ii) selecting a cut point (iii) splitting and merging, and (iv) determining termination condition.

1.3.1 Classification of Discretization Methods

Discretization can be classified into the following ways [62]:

(i)   Supervised and unsupervised
(ii) Local and global
(iii) Static and Dynamic
(iv) Error-based and entropy-based
(v)   Top-down and bottom-up.

When class labels of the objects are not known, discretization is referred to as *unsupervised* methods [63], while discretization in the presence of class labels is referred to as *supervised* methods [64].

Local discretization methods [65] partition continuous data in localized regions in the instance space. In decision tree building process [66], local discretization method is used. On the other hand, *global* discretization methods [67] discretize continuous attribute values considering total domain space.

Partitioning, while done independent of other features, is called *static* [68] while all features are discretized simultaneously, called *dynamic* discretizing [68].

Minimum error due to discretization is referred as *error-based* methods [69]. In *entropy-based* methods [69], class information entropy of the candidates present in the intervals is used to determine the threshold for obtaining the interval boundaries.

Defining a large interval with all values is the starting step of *top-down* methods [28]. The method detects the cut points recursively and terminates based on some defined criteria. *Bottom-up* methods [28] work in the reverse way of *top-down* methods. In this method, small intervals are combined to form a large interval to meet the desired criteria.

1.3.2   Methods of Discretization

1.3.2.1   Equal Width

In the binning process of discretization, attributes with continuous values are distributed into a fixed number of bins. In the equal width discretization algorithm (EWDA), the width of the bins is equal. Highest and lowest values of the discretized attributes are determined by the EWDA. In this algorithm, the range of continuous attribute is divided into equal width discrete intervals, as specified by the users. EWDA fails to deliver desirable outcome when continuous attribute values are not evenly distributed, resulting in loss of information due to discretization of attributes.

1.3.2.2   Equal Frequency

In equal frequency discretization algorithm (EFDA) [70], continuous attribute values are kept in the specified number of bins, maintaining equal frequency interval. Here, the attributes are sorted in ascending order, considering maximum and minimum range of attribute values.

1.3.2.3   Bottom-up Merging

At the beginning of bottom-up merging process [28], arbitrary number of intervals for continuous attributes is considered. Similarity, test is conducted for the adjacent intervals. If similarity measure is greater than the predefined target value, then merging of those intervals is performed to form a new interval. The process of forming new intervals is continued till all intervals become dissimilar considering the defined similarity measure.

1.3.2.4   ChiMerge

ChiMerge procedure [71, 72] is applied to merge the intervals heuristically, which are adjacent, as tested using the class frequency value. Initially, every instance is considered as an interval for discretization. We calculate χ^2 value considering each pair of intervals. Intervals which are adjacent keep on merging till each χ^2 value is greater than a predefined threshold. The algorithm terminates by merging distinct adjacent intervals, as tested by χ^2 value.

1.3.2.5 Entropy Based

Continuous attributes are discretized by entropy-based method [73] using minimal entropy heuristic [69]. Based on minimum entropy value, cuts are applied recursively, which may be binary or multiple. The process terminates depending on the number of cuts which are predefined, or information gain or minimum description length principle (MDLP) [74]. ID3 method [75] uses Shanon's entropy measure [76] for discretization, which is based on inductive approach using decision tree knowledge. ID3 uses greedy approach to obtain the prospective cut points considering the span of values of continuous attributes. The range is split using the cut point having lowest entropy value. Each part is further split, and the method continues till a predefined stopping criterion is achieved. The approach belongs to the category which uses local information supervised in nature and dynamic.

Entropy/MDL [70] is an algorithm that recursively partitioned the values of each attribute, results optimization of entropy as local measures. In the algorithm, the stopping criterion for partitioning is defined using MDL principle.

Class-Attribute Dependent Discretizer (CADD): This method [77] exploits class-attribute dependency concept, by maximizing the relation between classes and attributes. The approach estimates joint probability of belongingness of an object into a particular class with attribute value in a predefined range.

1.3.2.6 Nonparameterized Supervised Discretization

Unparameterized Supervised Discretization procedure [78] aims at obtaining the highest goodness of an interval by preserving the content of information that lies in the continuous attribute. *Goodness* of ith interval (I_i) is expressed below, evaluating connection among goal and error of ith interval.

$$Goodness(I_i) = \frac{goals(I_i)}{1 + errors(I_i)}$$

This nonparametric method calculates the intervals by maximizing interval purity. For very large number of intervals, the algorithm merges the intervals, provided union of two goodness is higher than average goodness of intervals. This method is localized, supervised, and static.

1.4   Learning Classifier

Machine learning [79–81] aims at autonomously acquiring and integrating knowledge to continuously improve performance of task by applying experience and completing those tasks efficiently and effectively. Supervised [82–86], unsupervised [87–91], and reinforcement [92–94] are three main learning techniques used to train the machines.

Supervised and unsupervised learning have established their importance to various applications in industry and academics. In supervised learning, environment is learnt where input and target output sets are provided to train the system. In unsupervised learning, no target output is supplied, and the system learns by discovering relationship among the inputs. Reinforcement learning lies between supervised and unsupervised learning, where a measure of reward/penalty is provided by a critic. Supervised learning is mostly used but has a limitation to learn through interactions. The challenge to learn the environment by agents executing states, actions, and goals is possible using reinforcement learning (RL) technique. Prediction in case of dynamic environment is more suitable using RL in comparison with supervised learning.

1.4.1   Dynamic Learning

Reinforcement learning algorithms are applied on either recurrent or nonrecurrent neural network [95] where the network is trained with "evaluative" feedback different from the supervised learning algorithms. The reward is used as evaluative signal [96] with the objective to maximize it by learning the mapping from situations to actions. To achieve the objective, the learning model discovers the action yielding maximum reward while trying to know the environment using trial and error search [96]. The main challenge that lies with the RL is to receive an evaluative signal, generated after a long sequence of actions. The solution is to develop a predictive reinforcement learning system.

Reinforcement learning is defined by characterizing a learning problem unlike other learning where learning methods are characterized. The main theme of RL is to acquire the environmental knowledge using intelligent agents which interact with the environment to reach to the goal state. RL is a goal-directed search algorithm where agents [96] interact with the environment which is often uncertain. Interaction is explicitly designed considering the problem as a whole. The agents take action to change the state and attempt to achieve the goal state using the reinforcement signal. Sometimes, the next reward signal as well as the successive reward signals is affected by the immediate action.

The key challenge of reinforcement learning is to find the trade-off between exploration and exploitation [93]. An agent needs to take actions that were learnt earlier and becomes effective in terms of reward. At the same time, new actions are explored by the agents. Exploitation of knowledge for achieving reward and at the same time exploration of environment to obtain more effective actions in future are the combined objective of RL. Both exploration and exploitation are required to pursue the task without trapping at local minima/maxima. For many decades, mathematicians have intensively studied the exploration–exploitation dilemma [93].

1.4.2 Dynamic Classification

Machine learning algorithms are able to tackle unknown situations with the help of past knowledge about the system. Such knowledge is used to automate and update the systems considering different perspectives. Therefore, the learning classifier system could be used within a Knowledge Discovery system.

Dynamic classification [97, 98] solves the problem of sequential classification where the data are by nature noisy, nonlinear, and non-stationary. It can tackle the data which are delayed and/or missing in the system. Dynamic classification models [99] handle these issues using generic state-space approach. Classifier using reinforcement learning has been considered as dynamic classifier as it can classify online/dynamic data entered into the environment. Temporal difference learning classifier, Sarsa [100], and Q-learning classifier [101] are considered as dynamic learning classifier. Here, the book includes different kinds of attacks and classifiers by Q-learning algorithm that explores learned knowledge in unknown model-based environment.

1.5 The Work

Intrusion detection [102–105] is an important activity in a system to maintain security [106–109] by protecting computer network from different types of attacks. The book mainly aims at developing anomaly-based Intrusion Detection System (IDS) by considering various issues and challenges that often arise while dealing with huge real-valued data sets. Mostly, signature-based approach [110] is used in IDS, where a pattern which is predefined is known as "signatures," and the goal is to find the events which match with the patterns. Attacks which are not occurred earlier, not detected by the signature-based IDS, even the difference is very less with the predefined patterns. Moreover, building of models for automatic intrusion detection is non-trivial. This is due to handling of enormous data related to network traffic, which has high chance of imbalance distribution, ill-defined boundary of two class labels, and dynamic behavior of environment, which need to be adopted as a continuous process. Fortunately, the bottlenecks are handled by intelligent methods, having ability to adapting, high inference speed, fault tolerant, and flexible with information content. Building IDS using machine learning algorithms increases system performance in detecting traffic data whether normal or abnormal.

Another major problem of the IDS reported so far is that they do not follow methodical steps while building a model, which detect misuse/anomaly inefficient way [111–116] with minimal computational efforts. The existing IDS uses features which are all not important to detect intrusions. The detection procedure is lengthy and degrades performance of the classifier because it overlooks more specific and case sensitive intrusion domain characteristics inherent in the data set. The book proposes a novel approach to develop automated knowledge discovery methods using different data mining techniques to build an efficient classifier to detecting intrusions either "*anomaly*" or "*normal.*" The proposed methods applied in the book aim to achieving maximum classification accuracy considering intrusion detection data set in particular. However, it is worthwhile to mention here that though the book mainly concentrates on network intrusion domain, the concepts developed are also equally applicable for other domains too. To judge the efficiency of the approaches, continuous domain data sets like hypothyroidism data set , pulmonary embolism data set , iris data set, and wine data set [117] are chosen in the book.

1.5.1 Contributions

- In most real-life cases, data set generally contains combination of continuous, discrete, and nominal type of data. NSL-KDD network traffic data set is considered to analyze 11,850 objects and 42 attributes. Here, total attributes are 42, among which conditional attributes are continuous (34), discrete attributes are (7), and 1 is decision attribute with two class labels, "*normal*" and "*anomaly.*" Homogeneity in the data set is obtained by converting nominal data into discrete data by applying hashing function [118].

- The voluminous data contain redundant attributes, and at the same time all attributes are not equally important to take decision. Therefore, it becomes inevitable to reduce dimension of the information system by selecting important features that effectively reduces complexity of the system. The information system may also contain similar type of objects which need to be eliminated and reduce computational overhead. Rough Set theory [119–123] has been used for downsizing (both column wise and row wise) the information table and applied on discretized data only. Discretization of data is used to bind the continuous data into finite set of intervals. Generating cuts, a widely used discretization method, has been applied in the book to partition the attributes with real values. After obtaining the essential cuts, the next step is to map them into appropriate intervals using the method, namely the centre-spread encoding. Machine learning-based discretization approaches are proposed in the book, one is unsupervised Optimized Equal Width Interval (OEWI) technique, and another one is supervised Split and Merge Interval (SMI). Results demonstrate that classification accuracy has not been affected after discretization of data sets.

- In discretization process, while attempting to assign discrete labels to continuous data, there is high probability of information loss that invites inconsistency (different class labels for same attribute values) in the data set. The proposed discretization methods efficiently handle inconsistency while generating finite set of values. In the cut generation algorithm, a heuristic-based approach, we proposed to generate sufficient number of cut points, distinguishing pair of objects which are discernible with respect to class labels. Thus, inconsistency in the discretized data set is avoided by the proposed cut generation algorithm. Optimal equal width interval (OEWI) is a discretization process where number of intervals for each attribute is optimized with respect to the number of inconsistencies appearing in the data set. In case of Split and Merge Interval (SMI) technique, consistency is preserved even after discretizing the data.

- After discretization of attribute values, concept of RST has been applied to select important attributes, sufficient to classify the information table. Reduced set of attributes, called *reduct*, effectively reduces dimensionality of the table and hence complexity of the system. A subset of conditional attributes is called *Reduct*, able to represent the information system. However, finding all sets of *reducts* is difficult and NP hard, since *reduct* is not unique. Researchers are involved to develop new algorithms [44, 124] to obtain *reducts*, which are appropriate. Concept of discernibility matrix of RST was reported in [125] for generating *reducts*. This has been adopted in the work. By applying absorption and extension law, we eliminate redundant attributes, and finally important attributes representing information table have been obtained. In another approach, the concept of attribute dependency has been proposed where tree data structure is used for implementation. Proposed method is computationally efficient than Quick Reduct algorithm [126].

- Dimension reduction based on attribute dependency technique is implemented using NSL-KDD data set. SVM [127–130] classifier is applied for classification of network traffic data. Confusion matrix [131] is presented to analyze the performance of the classifier, using accuracy.

- Dimensionality reduction on continuous domain has been proposed by integrating Fuzzy and Rough Set theory [132–143]. Here, Genetic Algorithm (GA) [144, 145] has been applied to obtain optimal *reducts* unlike Fuzzy–Rough Quick Reduct [126, 146, 147] algorithm, which stuck at local minima. The method has been verified using UCI repository data set also. Classification accuracy obtained using the proposed algorithm in continuous domain shows better performance compared to discretized data set.

- Instance reduction is achieved by integrating Simulated Annealing [148, 149] and Rough Set concept. An algorithm has been proposed by modifying Simulated Annealing Fuzzy Clustering (SAFC) method [150, 151], where objects are clustered with respect to each attribute. Among the clusters, most significant cluster is selected to classify the instances based on that attribute. By thresholding, redundant and less important instances are removed from the most significant clusters. The remaining instances show comparable classification accuracy with that of the complete data set.

- Q-learning [152, 153] is used by majority of the researchers in online domain. Extended version of Q-learning is proposed to obtain the cuts. The cuts are applied for achieving maximum performance of the IDS in terms of accuracy with respect to each attribute. The Reward matrix in Q-learning procedure has states represented by different cuts of conditional attributes and indicated by rows, while actions are represented by attributes, indicated by columns. Depending on the values of possible actions, the new data are evaluated to execute the best action (here *cut* on attribute) learnt by the proposed algorithm.

• The flat structure reinforcement learning (Q-learning) suffers from computational complexity with increase of number of state variables in the problem domain. Hierarchical Reinforcement Learning [154, 155] is designed to deal with such problem. The whole problem is subdivided into hierarchical levels so that curse of dimensionality can be avoided. The main aim of the proposed hierarchical Q-learning algorithm is to evaluate an optimal range for each linguistic label of the attributes in order to build a rule-base classifier that maximizes classification accuracy in detecting intrusions. Computational complexity in hierarchical Q-learning reduces with respect to flat structure Q-learning without sacrificing classification accuracy.

1.6 Summary

The book is organized into five chapters. Chapter 2 has mainly focused on data discretization as a preprocessing tool to building the classifier, which can efficiently detect intrusions by classifying network data either as *anomaly* or *normal*. Three different methods of discretization have been proposed in this chapter based on statistical and machine learning approaches. Information loss and in consistency in data are natural phenomenon of discretization process, and the proposed methods addressed the issues efficiently in this chapter. Chapter 3 explains challenges of dimensionality reduction and use of Rough Set and Fuzzy–Rough Set theory in dimension reduction. Genetic Algorithm is integrated with Fuzzy–Rough Set theory to obtain optimal *reduct*. While reducing dimensions of data, both discrete and continuous domain data sets are considered, suitable for different applications. Size reduction or object reduction of information table is described, and a method is proposed for the same in Chap. 3. Chapter 4 discusses machine learning approaches to build dynamic classifier. Modified Q-learning algorithm has been proposed which generates optimal *cut* to each attribute in order to accommodate online data for detecting intrusions. This chapter also describes another approach, Hierarchical Q-learning with Genetic Algorithm. This has been proposed to generate optimized linguistic labels of the rule set designed to build the classifier. Each chapter presents results and provides comparisons with existing methods to demonstrate effectiveness of the algorithms. Chapter 5 concludes by summarizing the work with limitations and future work.

References

1. Z. Yu, J.J.P. Tsai, *Intrusion Detection, A Machine Learning Approach*, vol. 3. (Imperial College Press, 2011), ISBN-13: 978-1848164475
2. M. Abdalla, X. Boyen, C. Chevalier, D. Pointcheval, in *Distributed Public-Key Cryptography from Weak Secrets*, ed. by S. Jarecki, G. Tsudik Public Key Cryptography—PKC 2009, LNCS 5443, (© Springer, 2009), pp. 139–159
3. U. Somani, K. Lakhani, M. Mundra, in *Implementing Digital Signature with RSA Encryption Algorithm to Enhance the Data Security of Cloud in Cloud Computing*. 1st International Conference on Parallel, Distributed and Grid Computing (PDGC—2010) (2010)
4. D.E. Denning, An intrusion-detection model. IEEE Trans. Softw. Eng. **SE-13**(2), 222–232 (1987)
5. M. Ali Aydin, A. Halim Zaim, K. Gökhan Ceylan, A hybrid intrusion detection system design for computer network security. Comput. Electr. Eng. **35**, 517–526 (2009)
6. D. Anderson, T. Lunt, H. Javitz, A. Tamaru, A. Valdes, Safeguard final report: detecting unusual program behavior using the NIDES statistical component. Technical report, Computer Science Laboratory, SRI International, Menlo Park, CA, 1993
7. A.H. Sung, S. Mukkamala, in *Identifying Important Features for Intrusion Detection Using Support Vector Machines and Neural Networks*. Proceedings of International Symposium on Applications and the Internet (SAINT 2003) (2003), pp. 209–217
8. L. Zhou, F. Liu, A swarm-intelligence-based intrusion detection technique. IJCSNS Int. J. Comput. Sci. Netw. Secur. **6**(7B) (2006)
9. S. Owais, V. Snasel, P. Kromer, A. Abraham, Survey: using genetic algorithm approach in intrusion detection systems techniques, in *CISIM 2008* (IEEE, 2008), pp. 300–307
10. P. LaRoche, A. Nur ZincirHeywood, in *802.11 Network Intrusion Detection using Genetic Programming*. Proceeding GECCO '05 Proceedings of the 2005 Workshops on Genetic and Evolutionary Computation (2005), pp. 170–171
11. Y. Lin Ying, Y. Zhang, Y.-J. Ou, in *The Design and Implementation of Host-based Intrusion Detection System*. Third International Symposium on Intelligent Information Technology and Security Informatics (2010)
12. N. Devarakonda, S. Pamidi, V.V. Kumari, A. Govardhan, Integrated Bayes network and hidden markov model for host based IDS. Int. J. Comput. Appl. **41**(20), 45–49 (2012)
13. J. Shun, H.A. Malki, in *Network Intrusion Detection System Using Neural Networks*. Fourth International Conference on Natural Computation (2008)
14. Y.-a. Huang, W. Lee, in *A Cooperative Intrusion Detection System for Ad hoc Networks*. Proceedings of the 1st ACM workshop on Security of ad hoc and sensor networks (2003), pp. 135–147
15. Y. Wang, H. Yang, X. Wang, R. Zhang, in *Distributed Intrusion Detection System Based on Data Fusion Method*. Fifth World Congress on Intelligent Control and Automation. WCICA 2004 (2004)
16. A. Abraham, R. Jain, J. Thomas, S.Y. Han, D-SCIDS: distributed soft computing intrusion detection system. J. Netw. Comput. Appl. **30**(1), 81–98 (2007)
17. R.P. Lippmann, A. Vitae, R.K. Cunningham, Improving intrusion detection performance using keyword selection and neural networks. Comput. Netw. **34**(4), 597–603 (2000)
18. Nsl-kdd data set for network-based intrusion detection systems. http://nsl.cs.unb.ca/KDD/NSL-KDD.html (2009)
19. G. MeeraGandhi, K. Appavoo, S.K. Srivatsa, Effective network intrusion detection using classifiers decision trees and decision rules. Int. J. Adv. Netw. Appl. **02**(03), 686–692 (2010)
20. D. Gamberger, N. Lavrac, S. Dzeroski, Noise detection and elimination in data preprocessing: experiments in medical domains. Appl. Artif. Intell. **14**, 205–223 (2000)
21. O.P. Rud, *Data Mining Cookbook* (Wiley Inc., 2001)
22. S. Chakrabarti, E. Cox, E. Frank, R.H. Güting, J. Han, X. Jiang, M. Kamber, S.S. Lightstone, T.P. Nadeau, R.E. Neapolitan, D. Pyle, M. Refaat, M. Schneider, T.J. Teorey, I.H. Witten, *Data Mining: Know It All*, (Elsevier, 2005)

23. E. Rahm, H.H. Do, Data cleaning: problems and current approaches, bulletin of the technical committee on data engineering. IEEE Comput. Soc. **23**(4) (2000)
24. M.L. Lee, H. Lu, T.W. Ling, Y.T. Ko, in *Cleansing Data for Mining and Warehousing.* Proceedings of 10th DEXA (1999)
25. Y. Haitovsky, Missing data in regression analysis. J. Roy. Stat. Soc. **30**(1) (1968)
26. S. Oba, M. Sato, I. Takemasa, M. Monden, K. Matsubara, S. Ishii, A Bayesian missing value estimation method. Bioinformatics **19**, 2088–2096 (2003)
27. M. Saar-Tsechansky, F. Provost, Handling missing values when applying classification models. J. Mach. Learn. Res. **8**, 1625–1657 (2007)
28. J. Han, M. Kamber, J. Pei, in Data Mining: Concepts and Techniques", Third Edition", The Morgan Kaufmann Series in Data Management Systems, ISBN-10: 0123814790), Morgan Kaufmann Publishers, 2011
29. Eibe Frank, Mark A. Hall, Ian H. Witten, in *Data Mining: Practical Machine Learning Tools and Techniques*, 3rd edn. The Morgan Kaufmann Series in Data Management Systems (2011)
30. M.H. Dunham, *Data Mining: Introductory and Advanced Topics* (Prentice-Hall, 2002). ISBN 0-13-088892-3
31. D. Hand, H. Mannila, R. Smyth, *Principles of Data Mining* (MIT, Cambridge, MA, United States, 2001). ISBN 0-262-08290-X
32. L.T. Jolliffe, *Principal Component Analysis* (Springer, Berlin, 1986)
33. W.S. Torgerson, Multidimensional Scaling. Psychometrika **17**, 401–419 (1952)
34. R. Fisher, The use of multiple measurements in taxonomic problems. Ann. Eugenics **7**, 179–188 (1936)
35. R. Jensen, Q. Shen, *Computational Intelligence and Feature Selection: Rough and Fuzzy Approaches* (Wiley-IEEE Press, 2008)
36. J.H. Friedman, J.W. Tukey, A projection pursuit algorithm for exploratory data analysis. IEEE Trans. Comput. C **23**(9), 881–890 (1974)
37. J.H. Friedman, W. Stuetzle, Projection pursuit regression. J. Am. Stat. Assoc. **76**, 817–823 (1981)
38. C. Bregler, S. M. Omoundro, in *Nonlinear Image Interpolation Using Manifold Learning*, ed. by G. Tesauro, D.S. Touretzky, T.K. Leen. Advances in Neural Information Processing Systems, vol. 7 (The MIT Press, 1995), pp. 973–980
39. M.A. Kramer, Nonlinear principal component analysis using auto associative neural networks. AIChE J. **37**(2), 233–243 (1991)
40. J.B. Tenenbaum, V. de Silva, J.C. Langford, A global geometric framework for nonlinear dimensionality reduction. Science **290**(5500), 2319–2323 (2000)
41. S.T. Roweis, L.K. Saul, Nonlinear dimensionality reduction by locally linear embedding. Science **290**(5500), 2323–2326 (2000)
42. Z. Pawlak, *Rough Sets—Theoretical Aspects of Reasoning About Data* (Kluwer Academic Publishers, Boston, London, Dordrecht, 1991), p. 229
43. Z. Pawlak, Rough set theory and its applications to data analysis. Cybern. Syst. **29**, 661–688 (1998)
44. R.W. Swiniarski, Rough sets methods in feature reduction and classification. Int. J. Appl. Math. Comput. Sci. **11**(3), 565–582 (2001)
45. Y. Zhao, F. Luo, S.K.M. Wong, Y.Y. Yao, in *A General Definition of an Attribute Reduct.* Rough Sets and Knowledge Technology, Second International Conference, RSKT 2007, Proceedings, LNAI 4481 (2007), pp. 101–108
46. C. Liu, Y. Li, Y. Qin, in *Research on Anomaly Intrusion Detection Based on Rough Set Attribute Reduction.* The 2nd International Conference on Computer Application and System Modeling (Published by Atlantis Press, Paris, France, 2012)
47. Y.Y. Yao, Y. Zhao, Discernibility matrix simplification for constructing attribute reducts. Inf. Sci. **179**(5), 867–882 (2009)
48. Y. Zhao, Y. Yao, F. Luo, Data analysis based on discernibility and indiscernibility. Inf. Sci. **177**, 4959–4976 (2007)

49. A. Murua, W. Stuetzle, J. Tantrum, S. Sieberts, Model based document classification and clustering. Int. J. Tomogr. Stat. **8**(W08), 1–24 (2008)
50. A. Vimal, S.R. Valluri, K. Karlapalem, in *An Experiment with Distance Measures for Clustering.* International Conference on Management of Data COMAD 2008, Mumbai, India, 17–19 Dec 2008
51. V. Torra, in *Fuzzy c-means for Fuzzy Hierarchical Clustering.* Proceedings of FUZZ '05 the 14th IEEE International Conference on Fuzzy Systems, 25–25 May 2005. ISBN: 0-7803-9159-4, pp. 646–651
52. M.W. Trosset, Representing clusters: K-means clustering, self-organizing maps, and multi-dimensional scaling. Technical Report 08-03, Department of Statistics, Indiana University, Bloomington, IN, 20 Feb 2008
53. A. Semana, Z. Abu Bakara, A.M. Sapawia, Centre-based hard and soft clustering approaches for Y-STR data. J. Genet. Genealogy **6**(1) (2010)
54. M. Setnes, Fuzzy relational classifier trained by fuzzy clustering. IEEE Trans. Syst., Man, Cybern. Part B: Cybern. **29**(5) (1999)
55. J. Gomez, D. Dasgupta, in *Evolving Fuzzy Classifiers for Intrusion Detection.* Proceedings of the 2002 IEEE, Workshop on Information Assurance, United States (2002)
56. N.R. Pal, J.C. Bezdek, On cluster validity for the fuzzy c-means model. IEEE Trans. Fuzzy Syst. **3**, 370–379 (1995)
57. D. Dembele, P. Kaster, Fuzzy c-means method for clustering microarray data. Bioinformatics **19**(8), 973–980 (2003)
58. J.C. Bezdek, in *Partitioning the Variables for Alternating Optimization of Real-Valued Scalar Fields.* Proceedings NAFIPS. 2002 Annual Meeting of the North American Fuzzy Information Processing Society (2002)
59. S.C.G. Kirkpatrick, C.D. Gelatt, M. Vecchi, Optimization by simulated annealing. Science **220**(1983), 49–58 (1983)
60. Y. Wang, Fuzzy clustering analysis by using genetic algorithm. ICIC Exp. Lett. **2**(4), 331–337 (2008)
61. B.I. Wohlmuth, in *Discretization Methods and Iterative Solvers Based on Domain Decomposition.* Lecture Notes in Computational Science and Engineering (Springer, 2001)
62. K. Das, O.P. Vyas, A suitability study of discretization methods for associative classifiers. Int. J. Comput. Appl. **5**(10) (2010)
63. G. Agre, S. Peev, On supervised and unsupervised discretization. Cybern. Inf. Tech. **2**(2) (2002)
64. Q. Zhu, L. Lin, M.-L. Shyu, S.-C. Chen, in *Effective Supervised Discretization for Classification Based on Correlation Maximization*", (IRI 2011), pp. 390–395
65. N. Girard, K. Bertet, M. Visani, in A Local Discretization of Continuous Data for Lattices: Technical Aspects, ed. by A. Napoli, V. Vychodil, (CLA 2011). ISBN 978-2-905267-78-8, pp. 409–412
66. H. Liu, F. Hussain, C.L. Tan, M. Dash, Discretization: an enabling technique. Data Min. Knowl. Disc. **6**, 393–423 (2002)
67. E. Frank, I.H. Witten, in *Making Better Use of Global Discretization.* Proceedings of the Sixteenth International Conference on Machine Learning (1999), pp. 115–123
68. J. Gama, L. Torgo, C. Soares, in *Dynamic Discretization of Continuous Attributes.* Proceeding IBERAMIA '98 Proceedings of the 6th Ibero-American Conference on AI: Progress in Artificial Intelligence (Springer, London, UK, 1998), pp. 160–169. ISBN:3-540-64992-1
69. R. Kohavi, M. Sahami, in *Error-Based and Entropy-Based Discretization of Continuous Features.* Proceedings of the Second International Conference on Knowledge and Data Mining (AAAI Press, Menlo Park, 1996)
70. J. Gama, C. Pinto, in *Discretization from Data Streams: Applications to Histograms and Data Mining.* Proceeding of the 2006 ACM Symposium on Applied Computing (2006), pp. 662–667. ISBN:1-59593-108-2, 2006
71. H. Liu, R. Setiono, in Chi2: Feature Selection and Discretization of Numeric Attributes. Proceedings of 7th IEEE International Conference on Tools with Artificial Intelligence (1995)

72. F.E.H. Tay, L. Shen, A modified Chi2 algorithm for discretization. IEEE Trans. Knowl. Data Eng. **14**(3) (2002)
73. R.-P. Li, Z.-O. Wang, in *An Entropy-Based Discretization Method for Classification Rules with Inconsistency Checking*. Proceedings of the First International Conference on Machine Learning and Cybernetics, Beijing, 4–5 Nov 2002
74. R. Jin, Y. Breitbart, C. Muoh, Data discretization unification. J. Knowl. Inf. Syst. Arch. **19**(1), 1–29 (2009)
75. R. Bertelsen, T.R. Martinez, in *Extending ID3 Through Discretization of Continuous Inputs*, FLAIRS'94 Florida Artificial Intelligence Research Symposium (1994), pp. 122–125
76. R. Butterworth, D.A. Simovici, G.S. Santos, L. O-M, A greedy algorithm for supervised discretization. J. Biomed. Inform. **37**(4), 285–292 (2004)
77. J.Y. Ching, K.C. Wong Andrew, K.K.C. Chan, Inductive learning from continuous and mixed-mode data. IEEE Trans. Pattern Anal. Mach. Intell. (1995)
78. R. Giraldez, J.S., Aguilar-ruiz et al., Discretization oriented to decision rules generation. Front. Artif. Intell. Appl. (2002)
79. T. Mitchell, *Machine Learning* (McGraw-Hill, New York, 1997)
80. J.-S. Roger Jang, C.-T. Sun, E. Mizutani, in *Neuro-Fuzzy and Soft Computing: A Computational Approach to Learning and Machine Intelligence* (Prentice Hall, 1997). ISBN: 0-13-261066-3
81. I. Czarnowski, P. Jędrzejowicz, Instance reduction approach to machine learning and multi-database mining. Ann UMCS Inf AI **4**, 60–71 (2006)
82. Y. Li, L. Guo, An active learning based TCM-KNN algorithm for supervised network intrusion detection, in *26th Computers and Security* (2007), pp. 459–467
83. A. Niculescu-Mizil, R. Caruana, in *Predicting Good Probabilities with Supervised Learning*. Proceedings of 22nd International Conference on Machine Learning (ICML-2005) (ACM Press, New York, NY, USA, 2005), pp. 625–632. ISBN 1-59593-180-52005
84. G.E. Batista, M.C. Monard, An analysis of four missing data treatment methods for supervised learning. Appl. Artif. Intell. **17**(5–6), 519–533 (2003)
85. S.B. Kotsiantis, D. Kanellopoulos, P.E. Pintelas, Data preprocessing for supervised leaning. Int. J. Comput. Sci. **1**(2) (2006). ISSN 1306-4428
86. S.B. Kotsiantis, Supervised machine learning: a review of classification techniques. Informatica **31**(2007), 249–268 (2007)
87. T.B.K.A. Bouchard-Côté, J.D.D. Klein, in *Painless Unsupervised Learning with Features*. Human Language Technologies: The 2010 Annual Conference of the North American Chapter of the ACL (Los Angeles, California). 2010 Association for Computational Linguistics (2010), pp. 582–590
88. Q.V. Le, M. Ranzato, R. Monga, M. Devin, K. Chen, G.S. Corrado, J. Dean, A.Y. Ng, in *Building High-level Features Using Large Scale Unsupervised Learning*. Appearing in Proceedings of the 29th International Conference on Machine Learning, Edinburgh, Scotland, UK, 2012
89. C. Liu, J. Xie,, J. Xie, J. Xie, in *Stochastic Unsupervised Learning on Unlabeled Data*. JMLR: Workshop and Conference Proceedings, 2012 Workshop on Unsupervised and Transfer Learning, vol. 27, pp. 111–122
90. J. Zhuang, J. Wang, X. Lan, in *Unsupervised Multiple Kernel Learning*. JMLR: Workshop and Conference Proceedings, Asian Conference on Machine Learning, vol. 20, (2011), pp. 129–144
91. T. Maul, S. Baba, Unsupervised learning in second-order neural networks for motion analysis. Neurocomputing **74**, 884–895 (2011)
92. L.P. Kaelbling, M.L. Littman, A.W. Moore, Reinforcement learning: a survey. J. Artif. Intell. Res. **4**, 237–285 (1996)
93. R.S. Sutton, A.G. Barto, in *Reinforcement Learning: An Introduction* (The MIT Press, 1998). ISBN-10: 0262193981
94. M.A. Wiering, H.P. van Hasselt, Ensemble algorithms in reinforcement learning. IEEE Trans. Syst. Man, Cybern. Part B **38**(4), 930–936 (2008)

95. W. Maydl, B. Sick, in *Recurrent and Non-recurrent Dynamic Network Paradigms: A Case Study*. Proceedings of the IEEE-INNS-ENNS International Joint Conference on Neural Networks, IJCNN 2000

96. C. Rodrigues, P. Gérard, C. Rouveirol, in *On and Off-Policy Relational Reinforcement Learning*. Late-Breaking Papers of the International Conference on Inductive Logic Programming (2008)

97. D.R. Lowne, S.J. Roberts, R. Garnett, Sequential non stationary dynamic classification. Pattern Recognit. **43**, 897–905 (2010)

98. S.M. Lee, S.J. Roberts, in *Sequential Dynamic Classification Using Latent Variable Models*. Advance Access publication on 27 Jan 2010, Published by Oxford University Press on behalf of The British Computer Society, 2010

99. S.M. Lee, S.J. Roberts, Sequential dynamic classification using latent variable models. Technical report, Technical Report PARG-08-02, University of Oxford, 2008

100. E. Even-Dar, Y. Mansour, Learning rates for Q-learning. J. Mach. Learn. Res. **5**, 1–25 (2003)

101. R. Dearden, N. Friedman, S. Russell, in *Bayesian Q-learning*. Fifteenth National Conference on Artificial Intelligence (AAAI) (1998)

102. Á. Herrero, E. Corchado, Multiagent systems for network intrusion detection: a review, in *Computational Intelligence in Security for Information Systems, AISC 63*, ed. by Á. Herrero et al. (Springer, Berlin, Heidelberg, 2009) springerlink.com ©, pp. 143–154

103. W. Lee, in *A Data Mining Framework for Constructing Features and Models for Intrusion Detection Systems*. Submitted in partial fulfillment of the requirements for the degree of Doctor of Philosophy in the Graduate School of Arts and Sciences (Columbia University, 1999)

104. W. Lee, S.J. Stolfo, K.W. Mok, in *A Data Mining Framework for Building Intrusion Detection Models*. IEEE Symposium on Security and Privacy (1999), pp. 120–132

105. A.L. Servin, Multi-Agent Reinforcement Learning for Intrusion Detection, Ph.D. thesis, The University of York, 2009

106. J.P. Anderson, in *Computer Security Threat Monitoring and Surveillance*. Technical report (James P. Anderson Co., Fort Washington, PA., 1980)

107. D.E. Denning, *Information Warfare and Security* (Addison Wesley Reading, Ma, 1999)

108. D.E. Denning, An intrusion-detection model. IEEE Trans. Softw. Eng. **SE-13**, 222–232 (1987)

109. S. Axelsson, in *Intrusion Detection Systems: A Survey and Taxonomy*. Technical Report 99-15 (Chalmers University, 2000)

110. K. Shafi, An Online and Adaptive Signature-based Approach for Intrusion Detection Using Learning Classifier Systems, PhD thesis, 2008

111. V. Chandola, A. Banerjee, V. Kumar, Anomaly detection: a survey. ACM Comput. Surv. **41**(3) (2009)

112. A. Lazarevic, L. Ertoz, V. Kumar, A. Ozgur, J. Srivastava, in *A Comparative Study of Anomaly Detection Schemes in Network Intrusion Detection*. Proceedings of the Third SIAM International Conference on Data Mining, 1–3 May 2003, San Francisco, CA, 2003

113. J.P. Early, Behavioral Feature Extraction For Network Anomaly Detection. CERIAS Tech Report 2005-55, Doctoral Dissertation, Purdue University West Lafayette, IN, USA (2005). ISBN:0-542-34849-7

114. R. Sekar, A. Gupta, J. Frullo, T. Hanbhag, A. Tiwari, H. Yang, S. Zhou, Specification-based anomaly detection: a new approach for detecting. Int. J. Netw. Secur. **1**(2), 84–102 (2005)

115. K. Wang, J.J. Parekh, S.J. Stolfo, in *Anagram: A Content Anomaly Detector Resistant To Mimicry Attack*. Proceedings of the Ninth International Symposium on Recent Advances in Intrusion Detection (RAID), 2006

116. T. Won, C. Alaettinoglu, in *Internet Routing Anomaly Detection and Visualization*. Proceedings of International Conference on Dependable Systems and Networks (IEEE, 2005), pp. 172–181

117. Uci: Machine Learning Repository. http://archive.ics.uci.edu/ml/

118. R.L. Kruse, A.J. Ryba, in *Data Structures and Program Design in C++* (Prentice Hall, 1998). ISBN-13:9780137689958

119. J.F. Peters (ed.), in *Transactions on Rough Sets XI*. Lecture Notes in Computer Science/Transactions on Rough Sets (Springer, Berlin, 2010)
120. J.F. Peters, A. Skowron, C.-C. Chan, J.W. Grzymala-Busse, W.P. Ziarko (eds.), in *Transactions on Rough Sets XIII*. Lecture Notes in Computer Science/Transactions on Rough Sets (Springer, 2011)
121. X. Ren, Intrusion detection method using protocol classification and rough set based support vector machine. Comput. Inf. Sci. **2**(4), 100–108 (2009)
122. Y. Caballero, R. Bello, Y. Salgado, M.M. García, A method to edit training set based on rough sets. Int. J. Comput. Intell. Res. **3**(3), 219–229. ISSN 0973-1873 (2007)
123. D. Slezak, G. Wang, M.S. Szczuka, I. Düntsch, Y. Yao, in *Rough Sets, Fuzzy Sets, Data Mining, and Granular Computing*. 10th International Conference, RSFDGrC 2005, Regina, Canada, Aug 31—Sept 3, 2005, Proceedings, Part I (Springer, 2005)
124. D. Deng, H. Huang, Dynamic reduction based on rough sets in incomplete decision systems. Rough Sets Knowl Technol LNCS **4481**(2007), 76–83 (2007)
125. A. Skowron, C. Rauszer, The discernibility matrices and functions in information systems, in *Intelligent Decision Support-Handbook of Applications and advances of the Rough Sets Theory*, ed. by Slowinski (1991), pp. 331–362
126. C. Velayutham, K. Thangavel, Unsupervised quick reduct algorithm using rough set theory. J. Electron. Sci. Technol. **9**(3) (2011)
127. S.S. Keerthi, S.K. Shevade, C. Bhattacharyya, K.R.K. Murthy, A fast iterative nearest point algorithm for support vector machine classifier design. IEEE Trans. Neural Netw. **11**, 124–136 (2000)
128. C. Cortes, V.N. Vapnik, Support vector network. Mach. Learn. **20**, 273–297 (1995)
129. V.N. Vapnik, *Statistical Learning Theory* (Wiley Inc., New York, 1998)
130. B.E. Boser, I. Guyon, V. Vapnik, in *A Training Algorithm for Optimal Margin Classifier*. Proceedings of Fifth Annual Conference on Computational Learning Theory (COLT-92), USA, 1992, pp. 144–152
131. B. Zadrozny, in *Learning and Evaluating Classifiers under Sample Selection Bias*. International Conference on Machine Learning ICML'04, 2004
132. R. Jensen, Combining Rough and Fuzzy Sets for Feature Selection. Ph.D. thesis (2005)
133. S.K. Pal, P. Mitra, Case generation using rough sets with fuzzy representation. IEEE Trans. Knowl. Data Eng. **16**(3) (2004)
134. Richard Jensen, Qiang Shen, Fuzzy-rough sets assisted attribute selection. IEEE Trans. Fuzzy Syst. **15**, 73–89 (2007)
135. R. Jensen, Q. Shen, in *Fuzzy-Rough Sets for Descriptive Dimensionality Reduction*. Proceedings of the 11th International Conference on Fuzzy Systems (2002), pp. 29–34
136. M. Yang, S. Chen, X. Yang, in A Novel Approach of Rough Set-Based Attribute Reduction Using Fuzzy Discernibility Matrix. Proceedings of the Fourth International Conference on Fuzzy Systems and Knowledge Discovery, vol. 03 (IEEE Computer Society, 2007), pp. 96–101
137. Hu Qinghua, Yu. Daren, Zongxia Xie, Information-preserving hybrid data reduction based on fuzzy-rough techniques. Pattern Recogn. Lett. **27**, 414–423 (2006)
138. R. Jensen, Q. Shen, Semantics-preserving dimensionality reduction: rough and fuzzy-rough-based approaches. IEEE Trans. Knowl. Data Eng. **17**(1) (2005)
139. R. Jensen, Q. Shen, Fuzzy-rough attribute reduction with application to web categorization, fuzzy sets and systems **141**(3), 469–485 (2004)
140. H. Guohua, S. Yuemei, in *An Attribute Reduction Method Based on Fuzzy-Rough Sets Theories*. First International Workshop on Education Technology and Computer Science (2009)
141. R. Jensen, Q. Shen, in *Rough and Fuzzy Sets for Dimensionality Reduction* (2001)
142. R. Jensen, A. Tuson, Q. Shen, in *Extending Propositional Satisfiability to Determine Minimal Fuzzy-Rough Reducts*. Proceedings of FUZZ-IEEE (2010)
143. R. Jensen, C. Cornelis, in *Fuzzy-Rough Instance Selection*. Proceedings of FUZZ-IEEE (2010)
144. E.P. Ephzibah, B. Sarojini, J. Emerald Sheela, A study on the analysis of genetic algorithms with various classification techniques for feature selection. Int. J. Comput. Appl. **8**(8) (2010)

145. M. Mitchell, *An Introduction to Genetic Algorithms* (MIT Press, Cambridge, MA, 1996)
146. Y. Rama Devi, P. Venu Gopal, P.S.V.S. Sai Prasad, Fuzzy rough data reduction using SVD. Int. J. Comput. Electr. Eng. **3**(3) (2011)
147. J.R. Anaraki, M. Eftekhari, in *Improving Fuzzy-Rough Quick Reduct for Feature Selection*. IEEE 19th Iranian Conference on Electrical Engineering (ICEE, 2011), pp. 1–6
148. S. Kirkpatrik, C. Gelatt, M. Vecchi, Optimization by simulated annealing. Science **220**, 671–680 (1983)
149. S. Bandyopadhyay, Simulated annealing using a reversible jump markov chain monte carlo algorithm for fuzzy clustering. IEEE Trans. Knowl. Data Eng. **17**(4) (2005)
150. X.Y. Wang, G. Whitwell, J.M. Garibaldi, in *The Application Of A Simulated Annealing Fuzzy Clustering Algorithm For Cancer Diagnosis*. Proceedings of IEEE 4th International Conference on Intelligent Systems Design and Application, Budapest, Hungary, 26–28 Aug 2004, pp. 467–472
151. N. Sengupta, A. Srivastava, J. Sil, in *Chapter 14 Reduction of Data Size in Intrusion Domain Using Modified Simulated Annealing Fuzzy Clustering Algorithm* (Springer Science and Business Media LLC, 2013)
152. C.J.C.H. Watkins, P. Dayan, Q-learning. Mach. Learn. **8**(3–4), 279–292 (1992)
153. S. Manju, M. Punithavalli, An analysis of Q-learning algorithms with strategies of reward function. Int. J. Comput. Sci. Eng. (IJCSE), **3**(2) (2011). ISSN: 0975-3397
154. A.G. Barto, S. Mahadevan, Recent advances in hierarchical reinforcement learning. Discrete Event Dyn. Syst. **13**, 341–379 (2003)
155. T.G. Dietterich, Hierarchical reinforcement learning with the maxq value function decomposition. J. Artif. Intell. Res. **13**, 227–303 (2000)

Chapter 2
Discretization

The process of transforming of continuous functions, variables, data, and models into discrete form is known as discretization. Real-world processes usually deal with continuous variables. However, for being processed in a computer, the data sets generated by these processes need to be discretized. There are many advantages of discretization [1–8]. Using discretized input data, higher accuracy of learning and better processing speed are achieved to produce the results in brief and comprehensive shape. Attributes, which are discrete, are easier to handle, interpretable, and understandable. But in data analysis, few negative effects come along with the process of discretization. Existing methods of discretization have some major drawbacks. One of them is loss of information in presenting the system, resulting in inconsistency [9] in data. Because of that classification accuracy is sacrificed.

Existence of vague and inconsistent data set among large data of real-life information systems is very common. While processing data of information system, Rough Set Theory (RST) [10, 11] is capable to handle such vague and inconsistent data to find knowledge [12–16]. This inspired us to employ RST as a data mining technique in this book. Generally, a real-life information system consists of continuous and discrete data. As RST [17] cannot accept continuous data as input, discretization is a necessary step of data preprocessing to make data suitable for RST. Loss of information takes place in discretization process due to approximation. Development of effective and efficient method of discretization is discussed in this chapter with the goal of minimizing loss of information keeping consistency in a compact way. To achieve this goal, two distinct discretization methods are discussed here. Primarily, we consider NSL-KDD network data set for application in the proposed concept of discretization.

2.1 Preprocessing

NSL-KDD is originated from KDD Cup 1999 [18], the old version of network traffic data set having forty-one conditional attributes with either real or nominal value. First nominal data are converted to real values using standard hashing algorithms [19], and

© Springer Nature Singapore Pte Ltd. 2020   27
N. Sengupta and J. Sil, *Intrusion Detection*, Cognitive Intelligence and Robotics,
https://doi.org/10.1007/978-981-15-2716-6_2

thus real homogeneity in attribute values is ensured. In statistics [20, 21], observations [22] may have different values. Some observations have values within normal range or have desired patterns and some have values beyond this normal range, either in positive or in negative side. Such observations are known as outliers. In NSL-KDD intrusion detection data set [23–28], outlier is considered to have the substantially large or small value of an attribute with respect to other values of the specific attribute [29]. Value of outlier is either very high or very low value. Due to this reason, while calculating statistical summary, like, mean, median, mode, variance, etc., of an attribute erroneous results are produced. Therefore, outliers have an impact on the performance of the classifier, which inherently relies on the statistics of the attribute set [30]. Statistically, we observe that majority of the distributions absorb all the legitimate statistical data within the range defined by $[(m - 4Xstd), (m + 4Xstd)]$ where m and std represent mean and standard deviation, respectively. The value of an attribute, if not within the span, is considered as an outlier and replacing the outlier from the data set is a necessity to avoid getting incorrect result. Value of outlier is replaced by the attribute's mean value. After removal of outliers, each feature lies within a statistically restricted span consisting of real values.

2.2 Cut Generation Method

Discretization has been done on data set to develop the coherence on the range of values of conditional attributes [31–35] which are continuous. Discretization method helps in observing and interpreting the objects and their corresponding classes, comparing the patterns of the values of all conditional attributes. Different discretization methods [17, 36, 37] are already available in the literature, but in practice, a particular discretization method is suitable for a specific area of application. In real-information system, the proportion of continuous variables is extremely large, and those variables are difficult to handle for its large dimensionality and size. To avoid this problem, the entire range of numeric continuous variables is partitioned into a few sub-ranges [38, 39] and each of these sub-ranges is known as a category. Each of these categories is associated with a definite decision variable. In this book, for network traffic data set, many continuous variables are considered as conditional attributes for "normal" and "anomaly" types of decision class. Relationship between the intervals of continuous variables and decision attributes ("normal" and "anomaly") is closely observed in this chapter. The main aim of this approach is to maximize the correlation between intervals of continuous attribute values and class labels, while the secondary objective is to minimize the number of partitions without affecting the relationship between decision class and interval values.

Mostly used discretization [40, 41] method is cut generation method [42] which represents optimal partitions of real-valued attributes. Cut point, with respect to a particular variable, is defined using Eq. (2.1) where maximum and minimum values of the same variable are obtained while number of partitions is assumed.

$$\text{Cut point}_{\text{variable}} = \frac{\text{max\_}value_{variable} - \text{min\_}value_{variable}}{number\ of\ partitions} \qquad (2.1)$$

In the proposed method of discretization, a group of cut points is created by using an exploratory method devised to discern each pair of objects in a distinct way. The discretization process is consisting of three sub-processes. Generally, the number of partitions [43] or the heuristic rule [44] to develop the partitions is provided by the user. Here, detecting number of discrete partitions is performed by the first sub-process. Discovering the width or sub-range of the partitions based on the entire boundary of the points of continuous attribute is the task of second sub-process. During the final sub-process, the points representing continuous attributes are depicted using values of discrete attributes.

2.2.1 Algorithm for Generation of Cut

Input: Decision Table
Output: Cut Points

Step 1: Observe the values of nth column of conditional attributes of a decision system table and organize those in ascending order.
Step 2: For every conditional attribute, collect the objects depending on the value of class labels representing decision attribute (s)/* for NSL-KDD data set, two values of decision attribute are considered, "*normal*" (i.e., $s = 1$) and "*anomaly*" (i.e., $s = 2$).
Step 3: Following rules are considered to identify the values of nth conditional attribute which are ordered:
A value is identified by "circle," if it is associated with an object having class label, "*normal*" ($s = 1$).
A value is identified by "asterisk," if it is associated with an object having class label, "*anomaly*" ($s = 2$).
Step 4: Examine the values of nth attribute which are identified by "asterisk" or "circle" in order to fix the cut points within the consecutive values (e.g., *at-n_val-5* and *at-n_val-6*) as described below.

Choose the cut which is the midpoint in the range [*at-n_val-5*, *at-n_val-6*] provided the value of nth attribute, *at-n_val-5* is identified by "circle" (or "asterisk") and the consecutive value of nth attribute, *at-n_val-6* is identified by "asterisk" (or "circle").

(i) First possible way is that value of one nth attribute (say, *at-n_val-5*) is identified as both "asterisk" and "circle" and the value of consecutive same nth attribute (say, *at-n_val-6*) is identified as either "asterisk" or "circle," choose the cut which is midpoint in the range [*at-n_val-5*, *at-n_val-6*] marked differently.

(ii) Second possibility is that two consecutive values of nth attribute (say, both *at-n_val-5* and *at-n_val-6*) are identified by "circle" and "asterisk," choose the cut as the midpoint of the range [*at-n_val-5*, *at-n_val-6*].

Step 5: Follow the above steps considering each conditional attribute.

Using the above method described so far, the cut point is obtained between two consecutive attribute values of a continuous attribute, for which values of decision attribute of an object will be different. ***Therefore, from the given training data set, such data objects which have different decision attributes for nth conditional attribute, establishes a discernible pair.***

Example 2.1 Assume Table 2.1 consisting of 21 data objects or instances, 1 decision attribute (*de_at*) and 3 conditional attributes (*co_at1, co_at2, co-at3*). There are two probable values of decision attribute (*de_at* = 1, denoting "*normal*" and *de_at* = 2, denoting "*anomaly*").

Data set of decision system of Table 2.1 has been used for application of the proposed heuristic-based algorithm for cut generation.

Table 2.1 Decision system

co_at1	co_at2	co_at3	de_at
13	1	1	1
0	2	2	1
0	2	2	2
7570	1	1	1
0	1	4	1
0	1	5	2
10	1	8	1
0	3	12	1
5	1	8	1
0	2	10	2
0	1	14	1
0	1	3	1
282	1	9	1
0	1	15	1
0	1	6	1
0	1	16	2
0	1	11	1
0	3	13	1
7951	1	1	1
0	1	7	1
0	1	17	1

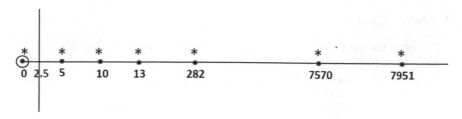

Fig. 2.1 Plotting of probable cut points for attribute, *co_at1*

The values of the attribute (***co_at1***) in an ordered way are mentioned as: {0, 5, 10, 13, 282, 7570, 7951}.

The result is plotted in Fig. 2.1.

Attribute, co_at1:

- Applying the above algorithm, only cut point derived is 2.5.
- Discernible pairs are: (0, 5), (0, 10), (0, 13), (0, 282), (0, 7570), and (0, 7951).
- Each of the discernible pairs contains two data objects, one element is taken from the set having single element {0} and another one is any value from the set with elements {5, 10, 13, 282, 7570, 7951}.

Similarly, applying the proposed algorithm for the attributes, *co_at2* and *co_at3*, the following cut points are generated as shown in Figs. 2.2 and 2.3, respectively.

Attribute co_at2:

- Applying the above algorithm, cut points are derived as: {1.5, 2.5}
- Discernible pairs are: (1, 2), (1, 3), and (2, 3).

Fig. 2.2 Plotting of probable cut points for attribute, *co_at2*

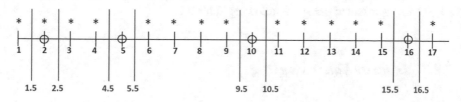

Fig. 2.3 Plotting of probable cut points for attribute, *co_at3*

Attribute, co_at3:

- Applying the above algorithm, cut points are derived as: {1.5, 2.5, 4.5, 5.5, 9.5, 10.5, 15.5, 16.5}
- Discernible pairs are: (1, 2), (1, 5), (1, 10), and (1, 16).

2.2.2   Encoding Method of Center-Spread Technique

Once cut points are generated for each attribute, center-spread encoding technique [45, 46] is used to encode the intervals. In the discretization procedure, the discrete value, which is the middle of the interval, represents the *center* of the interval consisting of continuous or real value. The variable *spread* represents range of real values for both sides of the middle point in discretized form. Therefore, an interval is expressed as (*center* and *spread*) [45] obtained using the following steps.

Interval Generation: An interval (*lower* and *upper*) is represented by two consecutive cut points where the interval includes the lower cut point (*lower*) and excludes the upper one (*upper*).

Center-Spread encoding: An interval is represented as (*lower* and *upper*) which is encoded as the *center* (middle point) and *spread* (range) of the interval. Here, the interval refers to the distance between the middle point and the end points at either side.

Example 2.2 Consider Example 2.1 and arrange the members of a set representing the cut points in increasing order. So, *co_at3* is written as: {1.5, 2.5, 4.5, 5.5, 9.5, 10.5, 15.5, 16.5}.

After including minimum and maximum values, we get: {1, 1.5, 2.5, 4.5, 5.5, 9.5, 10.5, 16.5, 17}.

Following intervals are represented from this set—

Interval # "1": [1, 1.5); Interval # "2": [1.5, 2.5); Interval # "3": [2.5, 4.5); Interval # "4": [4.5, 5.5); Interval # "5": [5.5, 9.5); Interval # "6": [9.5, 10.5); Interval # "7": [10.5, 15.5); Interval # "8": [15.5, 16.5); and Interval # "9": [16.5, 17].

After encoding by *center-spread encoding* technique, the intervals of attribute *co_at3* are represented using the following Table 2.2.

2.2.3   Discrete Value Mapping

The value of each attribute is positively lying in at most and at least one interval in *center-spread* encoding technique. In decision system, the discrete value of the continuous attribute is assigned as the corresponding *center* value of the interval in which the actual value of the continuous attribute is lying.

Table 2.2 Intervals using center-spread encoding technique

Intervals	Center	Spread
[1, 1.5)	1.25	0.25
[1.5, 2.5)	2.00	0.50
[2.5, 4.5)	3.50	1.00
[4.5, 5.5)	5.00	0.50
[5.5, 9.5)	7.50	2.00
[9.5, 10.5)	10.00	0.50
[10.5, 15.5)	13.00	2.50
[15.5, 16.5)	16.00	0.50
[16.5, 17)	16.75	0.25

Example 2.3 The center values in Table 2.2 are discretized as shown in the following Table 2.3.

Table 2.3 Decision system in discretized form

co_at1	co_at2	co_at3	de_at
3976.75	1.25	1.25	1
1.25	2	2	1
1.25	2	2	2
3976.75	1.25	1.25	1
1.25	1.25	3.5	1
1.25	1.25	5	2
3976.75	1.25	7.5	1
1.25	2.75	13	1
3976.75	1.25	7.5	1
1.25	2	10	2
1.25	1.25	13	1
1.25	1.25	3.5	1
3976.75	1.25	7.5	1
1.25	1.25	13	1
1.25	1.25	7.5	1
1.25	1.25	16	2
1.25	1.25	13	1
1.25	2.75	13	1
3976.75	1.25	1.25	1
1.25	1.25	7.5	1
1.25	1.25	16.75	1

2.3   Cut Generation Using Machine Learning Technique

Two different discretization methods are proposed in this chapter considering machine learning [47–50] technique. An unsupervised method, Optimized Equal Width Interval (OEWI) and a supervised method, Split and Merge Interval (SMI) [46] have been focused in the book. OEWI does not use the training set where set of conditional and decision attributes are provided to learn the system, it means that OEWI uses an unsupervised learning method, whereas SMI uses data from training set and test set to learn the system, in other words, SMI uses supervised learning method. It is noted that due to discretization, loss of information takes place which leads in formation of inconsistent rules and as a consequence, accuracy of performance results will be compromised. Therefore, minimizing number of inconsistent rules should be the strategy of these discretization methods. Handling inconsistency by these discretization processes is explained below.

2.3.1   Optimized Equal Width Interval (OEWI)

The discretization procedure partitions the span of conditional attributes into equal sub-range, known as Optimized Equal Width Interval discretization. Such sub-range is also termed as equal width (w) bins, as given in (2.2).

$$w = (v_{max} - v_{min})/k \tag{2.2}$$

Here, k denotes any positive integer, indicating number of bins, where $v_{\max}$ and $v_{\min}$ denote highest and lowest value of a continuous attribute.

Therefore, the value of continuous data is related to one of the sub-ranges or equal width (w) bins depending on their spatial distribution where each of the interval is having width (w) and the location of cut points are at $v_{\min} + w$, $v_{\min} + 2w$, ..., $v_{\min} + kw$.

Due to such discretization, values of conditional attribute which lie within a sub-range or an equal width (w) bins are mapped to a discrete value. As the bin size is pre-determined, inconsistent rules due to discretizing have been generated depending on k. Our objective is to obtain minimum number of inconsistent rules, which is achieved by applying particle swarm optimization (PSO) technique in OEWI algorithm in order to optimize number of bins, i.e., optimum value of k.

2.3.1.1   Particle Swarm Optimization (PSO)

While considering swarm optimization algorithms, PSO is the most popular for its simplicity in use, small code-length, and fewer control parameters. PSO employs a dynamics of particles with a tendency to attract members of the population toward three important points of interest in the landscape of the objective function. These three positions are popularly known as personal best position $\left(\overrightarrow{x}_{pbest_i}\right)$, global best position $\left(\overrightarrow{x}_{gbest}\right)$, and the direction of its inertial motion. Let $\vec{v}_i \cdot (t)$ be the velocity of a particle i located at $\vec{x}_i$. We then compute the velocity of the same particle at time $(t + 1)$ by

$$\vec{v}_i \cdot (t+1) = w\vec{v}_i \cdot (t) + C_1 \cdot \text{rand}(\cdot)\left(\vec{x}_{pbest_i} - \vec{x}_i\right) + C_2 \cdot \text{rand}(\cdot)\left(\vec{x}_{gbest} - \vec{x}_i\right) \tag{2.3}$$

where w is the inertial factor.

The position-update of particle i is given by

$$\vec{x}_i(t+1) = \vec{x}_i(t) + \vec{v}_i \cdot (t+1) \cdot \{(t+1) - t\} = \vec{x}_i(t) + \vec{v}_i \cdot (t+1) \tag{2.4}$$

The parameters w, C_1, and C_2 are used to control the response of PSO dynamics, i.e., solution $\vec{x}_i(t)$ of the dynamics given by (2.3) and (2.4). Here, w, the inertial factor, determines how much of the inertial vector $w\vec{v}_i \cdot (t)$ be contributed to $\vec{v}_i \cdot (t+1)$. Typically, w is set in [0, 1] for stability of the PSO dynamics. The parameters C_1, called swarm confidence, and C_2, called group confidence, are used to adjust the weights of $\left(\overrightarrow{x}_{pbest_i} - \vec{x}_i\right)$ and $\left(\vec{x}_{gbest}\vec{x}_i\right)$, respectively, to $\vec{v}_i \cdot (t+1)$. Effectively, Eq. (2.3) takes the resulting sum of three vectors: $\vec{v}_i \cdot (t)$, $\left(\vec{x}_{pbest_i} - \vec{x}_i\right)$, and $\left(\vec{x}_{gbest} - \vec{x}_i\right)$. The resulting vector $\vec{v}_i \cdot (t+1)$ and hence $\vec{x}_i(t+1)$ determines the flying direction and partition of the next search point on the search landscape. Figure 2.4a demonstrates the phenomenon of computing the resulting vector from the three vectors, as described in Eq. 2.3 (right-hand side).

PSO algorithm

1(a) Initialize $\vec{v}_i \cdot (0)$ and $\vec{x}_i(0)$ for $j = 1–M$, where M represents swarm population size.

(b) Initialize $x_{pbest_i} \leftarrow x_i$ for $i = 1$ to N.

2. Computation of $\vec{x}_{pbest_i}(t)$: Let $f(\vec{x}_i(t))$ be the fitness measure of $\vec{x}_i$ at time t. Determine $f\left(x_{pbest}(t)\right)$ and $f(\vec{x}_i(t))$.

If $f(\vec{x}_i(t)) < f\left(x_{pbest_i}(t)\right)$ then assign $x_{pbest_i}(t+1) \leftarrow x_i \cdot (t)$.
Do the above for all $i = 1–N$ particles.

3. Computation of $\vec{x}_{gbest}(t)$:

For N particles, we have N $x_{pbest_i}(t)$, $i = 1–N$.
Determine $f\left(x_{pbest_i}(t)\right)\forall i$ and find the largest $f\left(x_{pbest_i}(t)\right)$ among all members $i = 1–N$.
If the jth member has the least $x_{pbest_j}(t)$, i.e.,

$$f\left(x_{pbest_j}(t)\right) < f\left(x_{pbest_i}(t)\right), \; \forall i, \; i \neq j,$$

Then, assign $x_{gbest}(t+1) \leftarrow x_{pbest_j}(t)$.

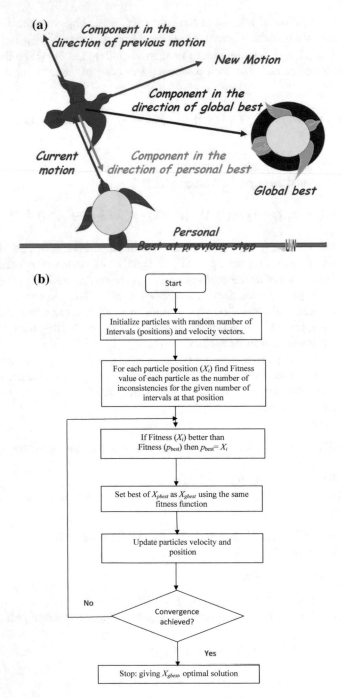

Fig. 2.4 **a** Particle swarm optimization, **b** flowchart of OEWI discretization process

4. Once $x_{pbest_i}(t + 1)$ and $x_{gbest}(t + 1)$ are known, we update $\vec{v}_i \cdot (t + 1)$ and $\vec{x}_i(t + 1), \forall i$ by (2.3) and (2.4), respectively.
5. Repeat from Step 2 until average fitness of all members in the current iteration t + 1 do not improve further with respect to the average fitness of the last, i.e., t-th iteration.
6. Repeat the best solution by presenting $x_{gbest}(t + 1)$, which is the optimal solution to the present problem.

In order to minimize inconsistency in the data set, it is used to design the fitness function of PSO algorithm and after each generation it is evaluated to assess the performance of the algorithm. So, EWO algorithm with PSO technique generates minimum number of inconsistent rules.

The concept of PSO is explained in Fig. 2.4a, b describes flow of the OEWI algorithm.

2.3.2 Split and Merge Interval (SMI)

Here,, discretization is done with respect to each attribute. Attribute having minimum difference in value discriminates the traffic belong to either, normal or anomaly class. Since distribution of attributes is different, so the specific range of values for each attribute is difficult to obtain. Homogeneous distribution of different attributes is achieved, as described in Eq. (2.5), which ensures that each value of different attributes belong to $[-1, +1]$.

$$std_{data} = \frac{average_{data}}{max(mod(average_{data}))} \tag{2.5}$$

The range $[-1, +1]$ is divided into number of finite intervals where length of interval is very small. Consideration of total range for splitting with very small interval, ensuring removal of inconsistency after splitting. In case, the presence of inconsistency exists before discretization, it is not removed by the SMI discretization method.

Large finite number of intervals are obtained due to splitting. Adjacent intervals are merged if corresponding objects belong to the same class label. Intervals are reduced while maintaining consistency in the discretized data due to the belongingness of objects in the same class label. It is worth to mention that the intervals are no longer remain same length. Data with non-uniform distribution and orientation are benefitted from SMI process, applied for discretization. Total range of data is transformed into intervals with respect to each attribute which is different and disjoint, eliminating inconsistency in data (Fig. 2.5).

The intervals are represented as $[-1, T1\delta v], [T1\delta v, T2\delta v], ..., [T(m - 1)\delta v, T(m)\delta v]$ where $T1 < T2 < T3 ... < T(m - 1) < T(m)$ and $T(m) = 1/\delta v$, the last interval.

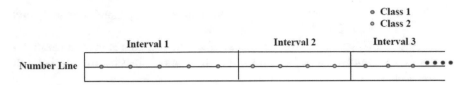

Fig. 2.5 Interval determination

Theorem 1 is explained to prove that the SMI procedure always maintains consistency in the discretized data set.

Theorem 1 *SMI discretization method always conserves consistency in the discretized data set.*

The theorem is proved by considering the first part as Splitting and second part as Merging proof is given in two steps, considering first the Split phase and then the Merging phase.

(i)   *Splitting maintains consistency in data set*

Proof Say, from splitting of an attribute we obtain $v1$ and $v2$, where $v1$ and $v2$ are distinct values belong to the same interval though representing two separate class labels. We assume, δu is the length of an interval, where attribute values with minimum difference exists and discriminating the two class labels. From the assumption, we can write $|v1 - v2| = \delta v \le \delta u$.

However, if two distinct class labels are denoted by $v1$ and $v2$, belong to same interval, their difference δv of course is minimum. Here, our assumption that δu representing smallest distance between two attribute values is not correct. Therefore, we can conclude that after splitting no such attribute values are obtained which belong to the same interval, but representing distinct class labels.

So, consistency is maintained after split step.

(ii)   *Merging maintains Consistency*

Proof Adjacent intervals, we consider for merging, provided the objects in the intervals belong to the same class label. Since splitting preserves consistency in data, so when we merge intervals with consistent data, consistency is preserved in the discretized data, as well.

Q.E.D.

The following example with continuous attribute value describes the SMI discretization algorithm using two-class labels (Table 2.4).

Two classes are separated when minimum difference in two attribute values (i.e., 0.30 and 0.20) is 0.10, Table 2.5 summarizes the data, obtained after splitting, which are consistent.

After splitting, merging phase processes the data and Table 2.6 shows the data which is consistent too.

Table 2.4 Example of SMI discretization process

Attr. value	Class	Attr. Value	Class
0.04	Normal	0.48	Normal
0.1	Normal	0.55	Normal
0.15	Normal	0.66	Anomaly
0.20	Normal	0.70	Anomaly
0.30	Anomaly	0.85	Normal
0.35	Anomaly	1.0	Normal

Table 2.5 Data after splitting

Span of Attr. values	Class	Span of Attr. values	Class
0.0–0.1	Normal	0.5–0.6	Normal
0.1–0.2	Normal	0.6–0.7	Anomaly
0.2–0.3	Normal	0.7–0.8	Anomaly
0.3–0.4	Anomaly	0.8–0.9	Normal
0.4–0.5	Normal	0.9–1.0	Normal

Table 2.6 Data after merging

Range	Class label
0.0–0.3	Normal
0.3–0.4	Anomaly
0.4–0.6	Normal
0.6–0.8	Anomaly
0.8–1.0	Normal

2.4 Discussions on Results

In the work, discretized data and actual real data of NSL-KDD data set [51] are used for classification. The discretized data set is achieved using the center-spread encoding cut generation-based discretization method. Results obtained with two types of data sets are compared considering different performance measures, like accuracy, mean absolute error, root mean square error, relative absolute error, and root relative squared error. Continuous attribute values from NSL-KDD data set are considered for discretization, using different classifiers and applying ten-fold cross-validation technique, accuracy is measured as plotted in Fig. 2.6. It is interestingly noted in Fig. 2.6, that there is very small difference in results of classification accuracies for different classifiers for discretized and continuous data sets and also to be mentioned that for some classifiers, results of classification accuracies are same for both types of data.

Table 2.7 provides classification and misclassification accuracy values with discretization and without discretization process using different types of classifiers and

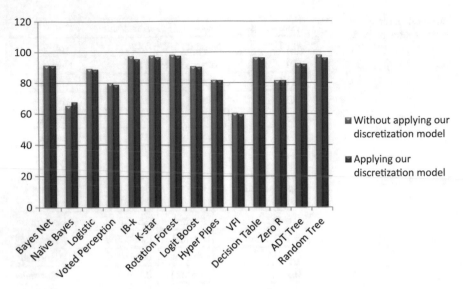

Fig. 2.6 Accuracy

errors. It is clearly observed from Table 2.7 that the difference in values for all the parameters (correctly classified instances, incorrectly classified instances, mean absolute error, root mean squared error, relative absolute error, and root relative absolute error), for both the conditions, (1) without applying discretization model and (2) applying discretization model, are insignificant. Similarly, by analyzing Table 2.8, we infer that data loss using the SMI discretization process is negligible.

2.5 Summary

In the work, heuristic-based cut generation method using center-spread encoding technique for discretization method has been employed for intrusion detection. Discussions on results and comparisons while using different error functions are provided for discretized and continuous data sets. Using the SMI discretization method, information loss has been minimized while maintaining consistency and integrity [52] in data. We conclude that unlike other existing methods of discretization, cut-based center-spread encoding technique does not generate information loss and maintains consistency in data. Classification accuracy has also been achieved with satisfactory result.

Optimized Equal Width Interval (OEWI) and Split and Merge Interval (SMI) discretization methods are mainly focused on handling inconsistency as proved in Theorem 1. In addition, they are equally good for minimization of information loss while applied on intrusion domain as depicted in terms of classification accuracy.

Table 2.7 Comparisons of classification accuracy and different error values

Classifier type	Classifier name	Without applying our discretization model						Applying our discretization model					
		Correctly classified instance (%)	Incorrectly classified instances (%)	Mean absolute error	Root mean squared error	Relative absolute error (%)	Root relative squared error (%)	Correctly classified instance (%)	Incorrectly classified instances (%)	Mean absolute error	Root mean squared error	Relative absolute error (%)	Root relative squared error (%)
Bayes	Bayes net	91.6292	8.3708	0.0947	0.2777	31.6533	71.7984	91.45	8.55	0.0926	0.2756	30.9917	71.2959
	Naïve Bayes	65.4765	34.5235	0.3437	0.5772	114.8573	149.2454	67.8	32.2	0.322	0.5597	107.7307	144.7744
Function-based	Logistic	89.3889	10.6111	0.1724	0.2892	57.6266	74.7825	88.85	11.15	0.1815	0.2975	60.7228	76.9517
	Voted perception	80.098	19.902	0.199	0.4461	66.5141	115.3422	79.01	20.99	0.21	0.4582	70.2482	118.5258
Lazy	IB-k	97.5998	2.4002	0.0244	0.1542	8.1485	39.8755	95.69	4.31	0.0436	0.2064	14.5953	53.3947
	K-star	98.0398	1.9602	0.0216	0.1184	7.2104	30.6053	96.91	3.09	0.032	0.1498	10.7198	38.7573
Meta	Rotation forest	98.4698	1.5302	0.0274	0.1046	9.1614	27.0503	97.74	2026	0.0384	0.1295	12.8411	33.4879
	Logit boost	90.8991	9.1009	0.1672	0.2708	55.888	70.0166	90.49	9.51	0.1643	0.2712	54.974	70.1568
Misc	Hyper pipes	82.0182	17.9818	0.4996	0.4996	166.9547	129.164	81.81	18.19	0.4998	0.4999	167.2072	129.2991
	VFI	60.6361	39.3639	0.4953	0.4957	165.5349	128.1652	59.86	40.14	0.4976	0.4978	166.447	128.7728
Rule-based	Decision table	96.6497	3.3503	0.0777	0.1686	25.9791	43.5849	96.5	3.5	0.0724	0.1692	24.2254	43.7776
	Zero R	81.6882	18.3118	0.2992	0.3868	100	100	81.71	18.29	0.2989	3866	100	100
Tree-based	ADT tree	92.5693	7.4307	0.1734	0.2499	57.9537	64.6075	92.22	7.78	0.1718	0.2499	57.4606	64.6543
	Random tree	98.2498	1.7502	0.0175	0.1301	5.8464	33.6285	96.34	3.66	0.0366	0.1895	12.2265	49.0291

Table 2.8 Comparisons of true positive, false positive, precision, recall, and F-measure values

Classifier type	Classifier name	Class	Without applying our discretization model					Applying our discretization model				
			True positive rate	False positive rate	Precision	Recall	F-measure	True positive rate	False positive rate	Precision	Recall	F-measure
Bayes	Bayes net	1	0.921	0.106	0.975	0.921	0.947	0.919	0.105	0.975	0.919	0.946
		2	0.894	0.079	0.718	0.894	0.796	0.895	0.081	0.712	0.895	0.793
	Naïve Bayes	1	0.616	0.17	0.942	0.616	0.744	0.649	0.193	0.938	0.649	0.767
		2	0.83	0.384	0.326	0.83	0.468	0.807	0.351	0.34	0.807	0.478
Function-based	Logistic	1	0.975	0.467	0.903	0.975	0.938	0.97	0.477	0.901	0.97	0.934
		2	0.533	0.025	0.826	0.533	0.648	0.523	0.03	0.798	0.523	0.632
	Voted perception	1	0.887	0.582	0.872	0.887	0.879	0.915	0.767	0.842	0.915	0.877
		2	0.418	0.113	0.453	0.418	0.435	0.233	0.085	0.38	0.233	0.289
Lazy	IB-k	1	0.986	0.069	0.985	0.986	0.985	0.978	0.139	0.969	0.978	0.974
		2	0.931	0.014	0.937	0.931	0.934	0.861	0.022	0.899	0.861	0.88
	K-star	1	0.989	0.058	0.987	0.989	0.988	0.986	0.105	0.977	0.986	0.981
		2	0.942	0.011	0.951	0.942	0.946	0.895	0.014	0.933	0.895	0.914
Meta	Rotation forest	1	0.99	0.038	0.991	0.99	0.991	0.987	0.067	0.985	0.987	0.986
		2	0.962	0.01	0.955	0.962	0.958	0.933	0.013	0.943	0.933	0.938
	Logit boost	1	0.976	0.389	0.918	0.976	0.946	0.974	0.405	0.915	0.974	0.944
		2	0.611	0.024	0.85	0.611	0.711	0.595	0.026	0.838	0.595	0.696
Misc	Hyper pipes	1	1	0.981	0.82	1	0.901	1	0.993	0.818	1	0.9
		2	0.019	0	0.946	0.019	0.037	0.007	0	0.813	0.007	0.014
	VFI	1	0.529	0.048	0.98	0.529	0.687	0.52	0.05	0.979	0.52	0.679

(continued)

Table 2.8 (continued)

Classifier type	Classifier name	Class	Without applying our discretization model						Applying our discretization model					
			True positive rate	False positive rate	Precision	Recall	*F*-measure		True positive rate	False positive rate	Precision	Recall	F-measure	
		2	0.952	0.471	0.312	0.952	0.47		0.95	0.48	0.307	0.95	0.464	
Rule-based	Decision table	1	0.988	0.128	0.972	0.988	0.98		0.988	0.139	0.97	0.988	0.979	
		2	0.872	0.012	0.941	0.872	0.905		0.861	0.012	0.943	0.861	0.9	
	Zero R	1	1	1	0.817	1	0.899		1	1	0.817	1	0.899	
		2	0	0	0	0	0		0	0	0	0	0	
Tree-based	ADT tree	1	0.977	0.303	0.935	0.977	0.956		0.969	0.288	0.938	0.969	0.953	
		2	0.697	0.023	0.871	0.697	0.775		0.712	0.031	0.838	0.712	0.77	
	Random tree	1	0.989	0.048	0.989	0.989	0.989		0.979	0.108	0.976	0.979	0.978	
		2	0.952	0.011	0.952	0.952	0.952		0.892	0.021	0.906	0.892	0.899	

References

1. Y. Yang, G.I. Webb, X. Wu, Discretization methods, in *Data Mining and Knowledge Discovery Handbook* (2010), pp. 101–116
2. A. Bondu, M. Boulle, V. Lemaire, S. Loiseau, B. Duval, in *A Non-parametric Semi-supervised Discretization Method*. Eighth IEEE International Conference on Data Mining (2008), pp. 53–62
3. I. Mitov, K. Ivanova, K. Markov, V. Velychko, P. Stanchev, K. Vanhoof, Comparison of discretization methods for preprocessing data for pyramidal growing network classification method, in *International Book Series on Information Science and Computing* (2010)
4. S. Bay, in *Multivariate Discretization of Continuous Variables for Set Mining*. Proceedings of the 6th ACM SIGKDD International Conference on Knowledge Discovery and Data Mining (2000), pp. 315–319
5. Y. Yang, G.I. Webb, in *Non-disjoint Discretization for Naive-Bayes Classifiers*. Proceedings Nineteenth International Conference on Machine Learning, Morgan Kaufmann (2002), pp. 666–673
6. C.N. Hsu, H.J. Huang, T.T. Wong, in *Why Discretization Works for Naive Bayesian Classifiers*. Proceedings of the Seventeenth International Conference on Machine Learning (2000), pp. 309–406
7. Ying Yang, Geoffrey I. Webb, Discretization for naive-Bayes learning: managing discretization bias and variance. Mach. Learn. **74**(1), 39–74 (2009)
8. Y. Yang, Discretization for Naive-Bayes learning, Ph.D. thesis, July 2003
9. R.-P. Li, Z.-O. Wang, in *An Entropy-Based Discretization Method for Classification Rules with Inconsistency Checking*. Proceedings International Conference on Machine Learning and Cybernetics (IEEE, 2002), pp. 243–246
10. R. Cang, X. Wang, K. Li, N. Yang, New method for discretization of continuous attributes in rough set theory. J. Syst. Eng. Electron. **21**(2), 250–253 (2010)
11. Y. Ge, F. Cao, R.F. Duan, Impact of discretization methods on the rough set-based classification of remotely sensed images. Int. J. Digital Earth **4**(4), 330–346 (2011)
12. C.-H. Lee, A Hellinger-based discretization method for numeric attributes in classification learning. Knowl. Based Syst. **20**(4), 419–425 (2007)
13. T.M. Cover, J.A. Thomas, *Elements of Information Theory*, 2nd edn. (Wiley Inc., 2006)
14. Z. Ying, Minimum Hellinger distance estimation for censored data. Ann. Stat. **20**(3), 1361–1390 (1992)
15. R.J. Beran, Minimum Hellinger distances for parametric models. Ann. Stat. **5**, 445–463 (1977)
16. I. Kononenko, Naive Bayesian classifier and continuous attributes. Informatica **16**(1), 1–8 (1992)
17. P. Blajdo, J.W. Grzymala-Busse, Z.S. Hippe, M. Knap, T. Mroczek, L. Piatek, A comparison of six approaches to discretization—a rough set perspective. Rough Sets Knowl. Technol. **5009**(2008), 31–38 (2008)
18. KDD Cup 1999 Data Data Set, UCI Machine Learning Repository. http://archive.ics.uci.edu/ml/datasets/KDD+Cup+1999+Data
19. R.L. Kruse, A.J. Ryba, *Data Structures and Program Design in C++* (Prentice Hall, 1998). ISBN-13: 9780137689958
20. F.R. Hampel, E.M. Ronchetti, P.J. Rousseeuw, W.A. Stahel, *Robust Statistics—The Approach Based on Influence Functions* (Wiley, 1986)
21. P.J. Huber, *Robust Statistics* (Wiley, 1981)
22. J.W. Osborne, A. Overbay, The power of outliers (and why researchers should always check for them). Pract. Assess. Rese. Eval. **9**(6) (2004)
23. C. Manikopoulos, S. Papavassiliou, Network intrusion and fault detection: a statistical anomaly approach. Commun. Mag. **40**(10), 76–82 (2002)
24. L.T. Heberlein, G.V. Dias, K.N. Levitt, B. Mukherjee, J. Wood, D. Wolber, *A Network Security Monitor*. Proceedings 1990 IEEE Computer Society Symposium on Research in Security and Privacy (1990), pp. 296–304

25. P. Barford, S. Jha, V. Yegneswaran, *Fusion and Filtering in Distributed Intrusion Detection Systems*. Proceedings of the 42nd Annual Allerton Conference on Communication, Control and Computing, September (2004)
26. S.R. Snapp, J. Brentano, G.V. Dias, T.L. Goan, L.T. Heberlein, C. Ho, K.N. Levitt, B. Mukherjee, S.E. Smaha, T. Grance, et al., *DIDS (Distributed Intrusion Detection System)-Motivation, Architecture, and an Early Prototype*. Proceedings of the 14th National Computer Security Conference (1991), pp. 167–176
27. J. Undercoffer, F. Perich, C. Nicholas, *SHOMAR: An Open Architecture for Distributed Intrusion Detection Services* (University of Maryland, Baltimore County, 2002)
28. R. Janakiraman, M. Waldvogel, Q. Zhang, in *Indra: A Peer-to Peer Approach to Network Intrusion Detection and Prevention*. Proceedings of IEEE WETICE 2003 (2003)
29. P.J. Rousseeuw, A.M. Leroy, *Robust Regression and Outlier Detection* (Wiley, 1987)
30. Janez Dem˘sar, Statistical comparisons of classifiers over multiple data sets. J. Mach. Learn. Res. **7**, 1–30 (2006)
31. C.-T. Su, J.-H. Hsu, An extended Chi2 algorithm for discretization of real value attributes. IEEE Trans. Knowl. Data Eng. **17**, 437–441 (2005)
32. F.E.H. Tay, L. Shen, A modified Chi2 algorithm for discretization. IEEE Trans. Knowl. Data Eng. **14**(3), 666–670 (2002)
33. V. Faraci, Jr., Discrete reliability growth tracking. J. Reliab. Inf. Anal. Cent. Second Quarter (2010)
34. W. Qu, D. Yan, S. Yu, H. Liang, M. Kitsuregawa, Kqiu Li, A novel Chi2 algorithm for discretization of continuous attributes. Prog. WWW Res. Dev. **4976**(2008), 560–571 (2008)
35. D. Tian, X.-j Zeng, J. Keane, Core-generating approximate minimum entropy discretization for rough set feature selection in pattern classification. Int. J. Approximate Reasoning **52**(6), 863–880 (2011)
36. Z. Marzuki, F. Ahmad, in *Data Mining Discretization Methods and Performances*. Proceedings of the International Conference on Electrical Engineering and Informatics (2007)
37. L.A. Kurgan, K.J. Cios, CAIM discretization algorithm. IEEE Trans. Knowl. Data Eng. **16**(2), 145–153 (2004)
38. S. Kotsiantis, D. Kanellopoulos, Discretization techniques: a recent survey. GESTS Int. Trans. Comput. Sci. Eng. **32**(1), 47–58 (2006)
39. R. Kerber, in *Discretization of Numeric Attributes*. Proceedings of the Tenth National Conference on Artificial Intelligence (MIT Press, Cambridge, MA, 1992), pp. 123–128
40. U.M. Fayyad, K.B. Irani, in *Multi-Interval Discretization of Continuous-Valued Attributes for Classification Learning*. Proceedings of the 13th Joint Conference on Artificial Intelligence (1993), pp. 1022–1029
41. R. Kohavi, M. Sahami, in *Error-Based and Entropy-Based Discretization of Continuous Features*. Proceedings of the Second International Conference on Knowledge Discovery and Data Mining (Menlo Park CA, AAAI Press, 1996), pp. 114–119
42. Xu Tan, Chen Yingwu, Half-global discretization algorithm based on rough set theory. J. Syst. Eng. Electron. **20**(2), 339–347 (2009)
43. J.Y. Ching, A.K.C. Wong, K.C.C. Chan, Class-dependent discretization for inductive learning from continuous and mixed mode data. IEEE Trans. Pattern Anal. Mach. Intell. **17**(7), 641–651 (1995)
44. Z. Ren, Y. Hao, B. Wen, A heuristic genetic algorithm for continuous attribute discretization in rough set theory. Adv. Mater. Res. **211–212**, 132–136 (2011)
45. S. Mazumder, T. Sharma, R. Mitra, N. Sengupta, J. Sil, *Chapter 62 Generation of Sufficient Cut Points to Discretize Network Traffic Data Sets* (Springer Science and Business Media LLC, 2012)
46. N. Sengupta, in *Security and Privacy at Cloud System*, ed. by B. Mishra, H. Das, S. Dehuri, A. Jagadev. Cloud Computing for Optimization: Foundations, Applications, and Challenges. Studies in Big Data, vol. 39 (Springer, Cham, 2018)
47. K.J. Cios, L. Kurgan, in *Hybrid Inductive Machine Learning: An Overview of CLIP Algorithms*. ed. by L.C. Jain, J. Kacprzyk. New Learning Paradigms in Soft Computing (Physica-Verlag, Springer, 2001), pp. 276–322

48. R. Giraldez, J.S. Aguilar-Ruiz, J.C. Riquelme, F.J. Ferrer-Troyano, D.S. Rodriguez-Baena, Discretization oriented to decision rules generation. Front. Artif. Intell. Appl. **82**, 275—279 (2002)
49. P. Datta, D. Kibler, in *Symbolic Nearest Mean Classifiers*. Proceeding of AAAI'97 (AAAI Press, 1997)
50. J. Ge, Y. Xia, in *A Discretization Algorithm for Uncertain Data*. Proceeding of the 21st international conference on Database and expert systems applications: Part II (Springer, Berlin, 2010), pp. 485–499
51. Nsl-kdd data set for network-based intrusion detection systems. http://nsl.cs.unb.ca/KDD/NSL-KDD.html (2009)
52. J. Han, M. Kamber, J. Pei, in *Data Mining: Concepts and Techniques*, 3rd ed. The Morgan Kaufmann Series in Data Management Systems (Morgan Kaufmann Publishers, 2011). ISBN-10: 0123814790

Chapter 3
Data Reduction

An information table comprises a set of data items, presented as tuples (rows), where each tuple includes a set of attributes. Data reduction refers to redundancy of both data items/instances and attributes, and thus is an important item of study in pattern recognition. Data dimension reduction [1] is contingent upon two conflicting issues: (i) selection of predictive features [2–4] for maintaining the proper class outcome in the classification problem and (ii) elimination of redundant information [5–7] with minimum data loss. Judicious selection of object instances in the information table also is an important concern. Selection of similar object instances thus also is important from the perspective of data reduction.

Two distinct approaches of data dimension reduction are introduced in this chapter. The first approach is concerned with discretization of data and later on using Rough Set theory. One basic problem of discretization is information loss. This information loss can be eliminated by utilizing the benefits of Fuzzy–Rough Sets. In fact, an algorithm for Fuzzy–Rough Set-based Quick Reduct (FRQR) computation is proposed for application in continuous domain data. Additionally, Genetic Algorithm is used in combination with FRQR [8]. The above mechanism offers a useful tool to choose minimum number of attributes, *reduct* [9] in continuous domain.

To test the feasibility of the proposed algorithm, a support vector machine-based classifier is employed to check the classification accuracy before and after reduction of attributes [10–12]. In case the classification accuracy, represented as "confusion matrix" [13], remains same, for removal of attributes, the selected attributes are declared as redundant. On the contrary, if removal of one or fewer attributes causes an increase in classification accuracy, then those attributes are retained. The approach to select the set of attributes that optimize classification accuracy is to choose them one by one and test the accuracy. In case the accuracy falls off, the attribute is dropped, else it is preserved.

Besides attribute reduction, instance reduction is undertaken here using the principles of extended Simulated Annealing Fuzzy Clustering (SAFC) [14] and RST. The following main steps are employed to perform the given instance reduction. First, an extended SAFC algorithm is employed to make partition between the objects considering values of attributes. Next, the attribute-dependency concept of RST is

© Springer Nature Singapore Pte Ltd. 2020
N. Sengupta and J. Sil, *Intrusion Detection*, Cognitive Intelligence and Robotics,
https://doi.org/10.1007/978-981-15-2716-6_3

utilized to determine the most significant cluster of each attribute. Consequently, attributes with less significance are removed. In order to select the right instances, we consider the whole instances of same class as a group. In case dropping of one or more instances does not deteriorate performance (here classification accuracy), we eliminate those instances from the information table.

3.1   Dimension Reduction Using RST

In this section, we briefly outline the definition of RST, which will be required to understand the rest of the chapter.

3.1.1   Preliminaries of RST

A decision table comprises objects and attributes along with values of the attributes where each object is represented by 3-tuple (X, ATT, V_a). Here, a non-empty set X, consisting of a particular domain of objects, is called universe of discourse. The non-empty set ATT contains different attributes, where V_a represents attribute value. Formally, for each $a \in ATT$, we have a mapping $a : X \rightarrow V_a$. We partition the set of attributes ATT into two subsets—the members of a subset are conditional attributes, CAT, while another subset with DAT, describing class labels of objects.

Relation
Suppose A and B are sets, defined on a universe X, where $x \in A$ and $y \in B$. We select R to be a relation between x, y satisfying certain condition. For example, suppose we need to determine the relation between $x \in A$ and $y \in B$ using $<$ operator, i.e., $(x, y) \in R$ if $x < y$. Finally, we can have

$$R = \{(x, y)\} : x \in A, y \in B, x < y$$

For example, consider an integer set of universe I. Let $A = \{2,3,5\}$ and $B = \{4,6,7\}$. We need to determine the relation R between $x \in A$ and $y \in B$ with respect to the relational operator
$x < y$. Then

$$R = \{(2, 4), (2, 6), (2, 7), (3, 4), (3, 6), (3, 7), (5, 6), (5, 7)\}$$

It is important to note that

$$R \subseteq AXB$$

For example, $AXB = \{(2,4),(2,6),(2,7),(3,4),(3,6),(3,7),(5,4),(5,6),(5,7)\}$

Equivalent Relation

The relation over a given set A is called an equivalence relation; provided conditions given below are satisfied.

1. If aRa holds with respect to the relational operator R for $a \in A$, then R is called reflexive.
2. For $a, b \in A$, if aRb and bRa, we define the relation is symmetric.
3. For $a, b, c \in A$, if aRb and bRc then aRc. True for transitive relation R.

Equivalence Class

For a given set A, and each element, $a \in A$ if

$$B_\alpha = \{x : (x, \alpha) \in R\}$$

Then, the set B_α is called equivalence class determined by α, where R denotes the equivalence relation. The set of equivalent classes $\{B_\alpha\}_{\alpha \in A}$, represented by A/R, is called the equivalent set.

For example, let $x, y \in A$ $universe$ X. Let $x \equiv y \bmod 5$, where mod denotes the modulo operation, describing the remainder in the division $y/5$. Since for any positive/negative integer y, $y \bmod 5$ can have five values: 0, 1, 2, 3, and 4, we have five sets $E_0, E_1, E_2, ..., E_n$, where E_i is the set of elements returning i after $y \bmod 5$ operation.

For example, let $E_0 = \{----. -10, -5, 0, 5, 10, ----\}$; it may be noted that for $E_0 = \{y \bmod 5\}$ and $y \bmod 5$ returns 0 for all elements of E_0. Similarly, $E_4 = \{-----, -6, -1, 4, 9, 14, ---\}$, $y \bmod 5$ returns 4. Here, $E_0, E_1, E_2, E_3,$ and E_4 are five equivalence classes.

Indiscernibility Relation

The *Indiscernibility relation* is often used in Rough Sets to declare equivalence between a pair of objects. Given two objects, x and y, the indiscernibility relation $IND(P)$, for $P \subseteq ATT$ is defined formally as

$$IND(P) = \{(x, y) \in X^2 | \forall a \in P, \; such \, that \, a(x) = a(y)\} \qquad (3.1)$$

P-indiscernibility relation is symbolized as *IND(P)*, and the *indiscernible* objects corresponding to P is represented by $[x]_P$. The subset of X, satisfying indiscernibility relation, is written as $X/IND(P)$.

Approximations

Approximations of set Y are denoted by *lower approximation* (*positive region*) and *upper approximation (possible region)* sets, which are crisp sets.

Fig. 3.1 Presentation of
rough set $\underline{P}Y$, $\overline{PY}$

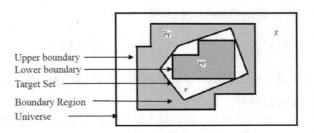

Upper boundary
Lower boundary
Target Set
Boundary Region
Universe

Lower Approximation

Given a target set Y, consisting of objects with attribute set P, we define

$$\underline{P}(Y) = \{y \in X, [y]_P \subseteq Y\} \tag{3.2}$$

as the lower bound $\underline{P}(Y)$ of P, where $[y]_P$ denotes the union of equivalent classes which are compulsorily a subset of target set Y.

Upper Approximation

For a target set Y, *upper approximation*, $(\bar{P}(Y))$, is represented by union of all equivalence classes in $[y]_P$. Intersection of such equivalence classes and set Y is non-empty. *Upper approximation* $(\bar{P}(Y))$ is represented with the possible elements of Y, given in Eq. (3.3).

$$\bar{P}(Y) = \{y \in X, [y]_P \cap Y \neq \Phi\} \tag{3.3}$$

Boundary Region

The annulus between upper and lower approximations of the target set Y is called the *boundary region* [1].

Rough Set (RS)

A Rough Set is defined as $\langle \underline{P}Y, \bar{P}Y \rangle$, shown in Fig. 3.1.

Positive Region

Set S contains decision attributes where conditional set of attributes is P. Then, positive region of a set Y includes elements essentially lies in Y. Finally,

$$POS_P(S) = X_{Y \in X/S}\underline{P}(Y) \tag{3.4}$$

where $POS_P(S)$ denotes a positive region containing all the elements of X which are uniquely classified for S decision attributes, considering the conditional set of attributes, P.

Attribute Dependency

In real-life decision system, many conditional attributes do not have any relationship with decision attributes. Finding dependencies between conditional and decision attributes is an important aspect of data analysis. Dependency is referred as the phenomenon that the values of conditional attributes determine the values of decision

Table 3.1 Decision system

Objects	Attributes					
	Conditional					Decision
	v	w	x	y	z	S
Ob_1	0	1	2	0	2	s_1
Ob_2	0	1	2	0	2	s_1
Ob_3	1	2	2	0	1	s_2
Ob_4	2	2	0	1	0	s_3
Ob_5	1	0	1	0	2	s_2
Ob_6	2	2	0	1	1	s_1
Ob_7	1	2	2	0	1	s_2
Ob_8	2	0	1	1	0	s_3
Ob_9	1	0	1	0	1	s_1
Ob_{10}	1	2	2	0	1	s_2

attributes. Let P and S denote the set of conditional attributes and decision attributes respectively, where S is completely dependent on P, dependency of S on P is represented as $P \Rightarrow S$. Dependency of S on P is measured with the degree k, which is symbolized as $P \Rightarrow_k S$ and defined using Eq. (3.5).

$$k = \gamma(P, S) = \frac{\sum_{i=1}^{L} |\underline{P}S_i|}{|X|} = \frac{|(POS_P(S))|}{|X|} \tag{3.5}$$

where $POS_P(S)$ is called a *positive region* as explained above and L denotes different class labels, as members of set S.

Degree of dependency (k) of S on P, i.e., varies between 0 and 1. $k = 1$ represents maximum dependency, and $k = 0$ denotes S which does not depend on P. Degree of dependency, k, denotes the significance of the conditional attribute(s). Greater value of k represents higher significance of the attribute.

For example, decision system Table 3.1 is given below to explain the concept of Rough Set theory.

3.1.2 Reduct Using Discernibility Matrix

Real-life decision system contains attributes, out of which some attributes are important for the system which contributes in deriving knowledge [15] and some are not participating in producing any knowledge about the system. Eliminating the less important attributes does not affect the integrity of the system rather it is essential to make the computation efficient. Therefore, it is important to discover the subset of attributes which help in deriving knowledge from the system in efficient way. Such set of attributes are called *reducts*. There are many ways to find these *reducts*.

As introduced before, a decision system is represented by a set of data points, each containing n attributes including corresponding class information. Let the attributes be $A_0, A_1, A_2, ..., A_{n-1}, A_n$, where A_0 through A_{n-1} represent conditional attributes and A_n denotes the class information (decision attribute). We select the important attributes which are the subset of the attributes $A_0 ... A_{n-1}$ of the decision system. Suppose we select m of n attributes which together decide the class information. The selected set of m number of attributes is called *reduct*. The $(n$-$m)$ number of attributes does not provide any information about the class, and so eliminated to reduce data dimensionality. Thus, the *reduct* set retains indiscernibility relation of RST.

To form *reduct* using Rough Set theory (RST), discernibility matrix, conceptualized by Skrowron [16], is formed. Discernibility matrix is a matrix where the elements of matrix are formed with the attributes of the objects for which two objects are different. *Reduct* is developed for dimensionality reduction [17–21] of the system without sacrificing the integrity of the system.

The *discernibility matrix (DM)* is described below:

Consider the decision system, *IS*, is represented by X, the universe; *ATT*, set of attributes; *CAT*, set of conditional attributes; *DAT*, set of decision attributes.

$X = \{ob_1, ob_2, ..., ob_n\}$, where $ob_1, ob_2, ..., ob_n$ are different objects of the universe, X.

$$ATT = (CAT) \cup (DAT).$$

Elements (dm_{pq}) of the *discernibility matrix (DM)*, for a pair of objects (ob_p, ob_q), is defined by Eq. (3.6) below

$$dm_{pq} = \{att\text{CAT} : att(ob_p) \neq att(ob_q) \land (de\text{DAT}, de(ob_p) \neq de(ob_q))\} \quad p, q = 1, 2, ..., n \tag{3.6}$$

Elements (dm_{pq}) of *discernibility matrix (DM)*, for a pair of objects (ob_p, ob_q), is defined by set of attributes for which object pair ob_p, ob_q will be dissimilar. If the value of discernibility matrix element is null, it refers that the pair of objects (ob_p, ob_q) is same. The value of discernibility matrix elements $(dm_{pq} \neq \phi)$ refers that the pair of objects (ob_p, ob_q) is dissimilar. A *discernibility matrix DM* is symmetric in nature, i.e., $dm_{pq} = dm_{qp}$, and $dm_{pp} = \varphi$. It is clearly identified that the *discernibility matrix, DM*, is a triangular matrix, either upper triangular or lower triangular.

Discernibility matrix of Table 3.1 is represented by Table 3.2. The decision system has five conditional attributes (v, w, x, y, and z) and three decision attributes (s_1, s_2, and s_3). Values of conditional attributes and decision attributes [22] for each object are shown in the decision system Table 3.1.

Discernibility function $f(s)$ is presented using (3.7) considering discernibility matrix (DM), shown in Table 3.2.

Table 3.2 Representation of discernibility matrix (*DM*) for Table 3.1

	ob_1	ob_2	ob_3	ob_4	ob_5	ob_6	ob_7	ob_8	ob_9	ob_{10}
ob_1	–	–	–	–	–	–	–	–	–	–
ob_2	–	–	–	–	–	–	–	–	–	–
ob_3	{v, w, z}	{v, w, z}	–	–	–	–	–	–	–	–
ob_4	{v, w, x,y, z}	{v,w,x,y,z}	{v, x, y, z}	–	–	–	–	–	–	–
ob_5	{v, w, x}	{v,w,x}	–	{v, w, x, y, z}	–	–	–	–	–	–
ob_6	–	–	{v, x, y}	{z}	{v, w, x, y, z}	–	–	–	–	–
ob_7	{v, w, z}	{v,w,z}	–	{v, x, y, z}	–	{v,x,y}	–	–	–	–
ob_8	{v, w, x, y, z}	{v,w,x,y,z}	{v, w, x, y, z}	–	{v, y, z}	{w,x,z}	{v, w, x, y, z}	–	–	–
ob_9	–	–	{w,x}	{v, w, x, y, z}	{z}	–	{w,x}	{v,y,z}	–	–
ob_{10}	{v, w, z}	{v,w,z}	–	{v, x, y, z}	–	{v, x, y}	–	{v, w, x, y, z}	{w, x}	–

$$f(s) = (v \lor w \lor z) \land (v \lor w \lor z) \land (v \lor w \lor x \lor y \lor z) \land (v \lor w \lor x \lor y \lor z) \land (v \lor x \lor y \lor z)$$
$$\land (v \lor w \lor x) \land (v \lor w \lor x) \land (v \lor w \lor x \lor y \lor z) \land (v \lor x \lor y) \land (z) \land (v \lor w \lor x \lor y \lor z)$$
$$\land (v \lor w \lor z) \land (v \lor w \lor z) \land (v \lor x \lor y \lor z) \land (v \lor x \lor y) \land (v \lor w \lor x \lor y \lor z)$$
$$\land (v \lor w \lor x \lor y \lor z) \land (v \lor w \lor x \lor y \lor z) \land (v \lor y \lor z) \land (w \lor x \lor z) \land (v \lor w \lor x \lor y \lor z)$$
$$\land (w \lor x) \land (v \lor w \lor x \lor y \lor z) \land (z) \land (w \lor x) \land (v \lor y \lor z) \land (v \lor w \lor z) \land (v \lor w \lor z)$$
$$\land (v \lor x \lor y \lor z) \land (v \lor x \lor y) \land (v \lor w \lor x \lor y \lor z) \land (w \lor x) \tag{3.7}$$

The discernibility function is consisting of some terms which are connected by logical AND ($\land$) operation, where each term is consisting of either single element or multiple elements. These multiple elements in such terms are connected by OR ($\lor$) operation. The terms which are equivalent are removed in next step, and the following reduced discernibility function (3.8) is derived from the above function (3.7).

$$f(s) = (v \lor w \lor z) \land (v \lor w \lor x \lor y \lor z) \land (v \lor x \lor y \lor z) \land (v \lor w \lor x) \land (v \lor x \lor y)$$
$$\land (z) \land (w \lor x) \land (v \lor y \lor z) \land (w \lor x \lor z) \tag{3.8}$$

Expression (3.8) can be simplified by employing the well-known *absorption law* [23] of Boolean Algebra. For the sake of convenience of the readers, the absorption law is briefly narrated below:

Absorption Law: Given two Boolean variables, A and B, the absorption law is given by

$$A \land (A \lor B) = A$$

The proof of the above law is straightforward as outlined below:

$$A \land (A \lor B)$$
$$\equiv (A \land A) \lor (A \land B)$$
$$\equiv A \lor (A \land B)$$
$$\equiv (A \land 1) \lor (A \land B)$$
$$\equiv A \land (1 \lor B)$$
$$\equiv A \land 1$$
$$\equiv A$$

By employing the *absorption law* on (3.8), *discernibility function* is further reduced and achieved as (3.9) below:

$$f(s) = (z) \land (w \lor x) \land (v \lor x \lor y) \tag{3.9}$$

The expression (3.9) can be restructured to form the *reduct*. Such restructuring can be performed using following steps.

For three Boolean variables, A, B, and C, the expansion law is given by

$$A \wedge (B \vee C) = (A \wedge B) \vee (A \wedge C) \tag{3.10}$$

The following steps are now applied in (3.9) to obtain the *reducts*.

Step 1: Identify the maximally occurring attribute in (3.9); outcome of this *step* is x.
Step 2: Detect the term(s) in which the above variable does not exist; outcome of this *step* is z.

$$d(s) = (z) \wedge (w \vee \text{x}) \wedge (v \vee \text{x} \vee \text{y})$$

Step 3: Apply "AND" operation between the variable achieved from *Step* 1 and the term(s) achieved from *Step* 2; outcome of this *step* is $x \wedge z$.
Step 4: Remove the variable identified in *Step* 1 from the term(s) of expression (3.9) and connect those terms by applying "AND" operation; outcome of this *step* is $w \wedge (v \vee \text{y})$.
Step 5: Apply "AND" operation between the terms derived from *Step* 3 and *Step* 4; outcome of this *step* is $(x \wedge z) \wedge (w \wedge (v \vee \text{y}))$.
Step 6: Apply Expansion Law to achieve final *reducts*.
Applying *Step* 6, we get

$$(x \wedge z) \wedge (w \wedge (v \vee \text{y}))$$
$$\equiv (x \wedge z) \wedge ((w \wedge v) \vee (w \wedge \text{y}))$$
$$\equiv (x \wedge z \wedge w \wedge v) \vee (x \wedge z \wedge w \wedge \text{y})$$

Therefore, finally reducts are achieved as $\{v, w, x, z\}$ and $\{w, x, y, z\}$.

3.1.3 Reduct Using Attribute Dependency

In this section, we present one algorithm to compute *reduct* using the attribute dependencies of RST. Here, a tree-like data structure is employed to determine the minimal set of independent attributes (*reducts*). In the proposed tree structure, nodes represent a set of conditional attributes and edges representing attribute dependency of the parent node. Child nodes are the reduced set of attributes obtained from the set of parent node. Thus, along the depth of the tree, the number of attributes gradually is reduced until the nodes become singleton. The steps of the algorithm are outlined below.

3.1.3.1 Reduct Generation

Initialization: *Root node representing set of conditional attributes*

Step 1: Calculate *indiscernible* classes considering the set of conditional attributes (P) and decision attributes (S) by employing Eq. (3.1).
Step 2: Calculate positive region $POS_P(S)$ by applying Eq. (3.4).
Step 3: Compute dependency of the parent node $\gamma(P, S)$ with the help of Eq. (3.5).
//Parent node is initialized as root node
Step 4: Determine set of child nodes C_i $(i = 1...n - 1)$, from a given parent node by removing each attribute from the parent node, //where n is the number of conditional attributes in the set P representing the parent node.
Step 5: $P = P - x$, //where x is the distinct element of set P
Step 5: Calculate dependency of the set of child nodes $\gamma(Ci, S)$ by employing Eq. (3.5).
Step 6: If dependency calculated in *Step* 4 for each C_i is same as the dependency calculated in *Step* 3, then *Step* 7 is followed, else the path is aborted.
Step 7: Execute *Step* 3 to *Step* 6 till the tree height equal to n

Procedure of *reduct* generation for decision system Table 3.3 is represented by Fig. 3.2. The decision system table is consisting of ten objects and four conditional attributes (v, w, x, y), and decision attribute, S, has any of the two possible values (s_0, s_1). Values of conditional attributes and decision attribute for each object are shown in the decision system Table 3.3.

The domain of different attributes (conditional and decision) is given below:

$$v = \{0, 1, 2\}; w = \{0, 1, 2\}; x = \{0, 2\}; y = \{0, 2, 3\}; S = \{s_1, s_0\}$$

Table 3.3 Sample decision system

Objects	Attributes				Decision
	Conditional				
	v	w	x	y	S
Ob_1	0	2	2	2	s_1
Ob_2	0	2	2	3	s_1
Ob_3	0	0	2	2	s_1
Ob_4	2	2	2	3	s_0
Ob_5	2	2	2	2	s_0
Ob_6	0	2	2	0	s_1
Ob_7	0	0	2	0	s_1
Ob_8	1	0	2	0	s_1
Ob_9	1	0	0	0	s_1
Ob_{10}	1	1	0	0	s_1

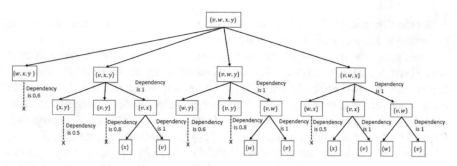

Fig. 3.2 Illustrating algorithm *Reduct*

Above *reduct* generation algorithm is evaluated step by step as explained below, where $\{v, w, x, y\}$ is kept at the root node.

Dependency of the root node is 1.

Attribute v is removed, and dependency for remaining set of attributes, $n1$, $\{w, x, y\}$ is computed.

Target set considering s_1 as decision attribute, we get $\{ob_1, ob_2, ob_3, ob_6, ob_7, ob_8, ob_9, ob_{10}\}$, and considering s_0 as decision attribute, we get $\{ob_4, ob_5\}$.

Considering *indiscernibility* relation, equivalent classes for subset of conditional attributes, $n1$, $\{w, x, y\}$ are $\{ob_1, ob_5\}$, $\{ob_2, ob_4\}$, $\{ob_3\}$, $\{ob_6\}$, $\{ob_7\}$, $\{ob_8\}$, $\{ob_9\}$, $\{ob_{10}\}$.

A total number of objects in the above equivalent classes are given below:

$\{ob_1, ob_5\} = 0 \, as \, \{ob_1\} and \{ob_5\} donotbelongtothesametargetset$
$\{ob_2, ob_4\} = 0 \, as \, \{ob_2\} and \{ob_4\} donotbelongtothesametargetset$
$\{ob_3\} = 1$
$\{ob_6\} = 1$
$\{ob_7\} = 1$
$\{ob_8\} = 1$
$\{ob_9\} = 1$
$\{ob_{10}\} = 1$

Total number of objects in above decision system $= 10$.

Cardinality of the positive region is calculated using Eq. (3.4) as below

$$POS_{n1}(S) = 1 + 1 + 1 + 1 + 1 + 1 = 6$$

Therefore, dependency of the attribute set $n1$, $\gamma(n1, S)$, is calculated using Eq. (3.5).

$$\gamma(n1, S) = \frac{|POS_{n1}(S)|}{|X|} = \frac{6}{10} = 0.6$$

As the dependency of the attribute set, $n1$, $\{w, x, y\}$ is 0.6, less than that of the parent node. So, this path will be aborted.

After removing w, x, and y from the root node $\{v, w, x, y\}$, child nodes achieved are $n2\{v, x, y\}$, $n3\{v, w, y\}$, and $n4\{v, w, x\}$, respectively. In the above similar way, dependency of child node $n2\{v, x, y\}$ is calculated and found as 1.0, same as parent node. Therefore, this path is proceeded further, and child nodes are found as $n21\{x, y\}$, $n22\{v, y\}$, and $n23\{v, x\}$. Dependency of each of these child nodes is computed. Dependency of child nodes, $n21\{x, y\}$, $n22\{v, y\}$, and $n23\{v, x\}$, are 0.5, 0.8, and 1.0, respectively. As the dependencies of child nodes, $n21\{x, y\}$, $n22\{v, y\}$ are not same as parent node, these paths are aborted. Therefore, one of the *reducts* will be $\{v, x, y\}$.

In the above similar way, dependency of child node $n3\{v, w, y\}$ is calculated and found as 1.0, same as parent node. Therefore, this path is proceeded further, and child nodes are found as $n31\{w, y\}$, $n32\{v, y\}$, and $n33\{v, w\}$. Dependency of each of these child nodes is computed. Dependency of child nodes, $n31\{w, y\}$, $n32\{v, y\}$, and $n33\{v, w\}$ are 0.6, 0.8, and 1.0, respectively. As the dependencies of child nodes, $n31\{w, y\}$, $n32\{v, y\}$ are not same as parent node, these paths are aborted. Therefore, one of the *reducts* will be $\{v, w, y\}$. Similarly, another *reduct* is found as $\{v, w, x\}$.

Therefore, the *reducts* will be $\{v, x, y\}$, $\{w, v, y\}$, and $\{v, w, x\}$.

Well-known Quick Reduct method [24] also shows similar result as that of tree structure.

3.2   Dimension Reduction Using Fuzzy–Rough Set

For dimensionality reduction in continuous domain, Fuzzy–Rough Set-based [25–28] method has been applied and the *reducts* obtained by this approach are optimized using Genetic Algorithm (GA). The proposed method has been verified on different data sets to prove its effectiveness in selecting attributes. We now briefly outline the foundation of Fuzzy–Rough Sets.

3.2.1   Fuzzy–Rough Sets

Vague information has been dealt using computational intelligent techniques, like Fuzzy Sets [29] and Rough Set theory [30] which are useful to solve many real-world problems. However, both the tools have their distinct approaches to uncertainty management. Fuzzy Sets usually are attributed by membership functions, and thus, continuous variables can be modeled in Fuzzy Sets by suitably selected membership functions [31–33]. Choice of membership functions in Fuzzy Sets is detrimental to the performance of approximate reasoning undertaken by Fuzzy sets. Rough Sets, however, do not require membership functions for its representations. Rather, it deals with discrete data only, even though the real-world data is usually continuous. In this chapter, we made an attempt to obtain the synergistic benefits of RST and Fuzzy sets [34, 35]. The resulting set is referred to as Fuzzy–Rough Sets. The Fuzzy–Rough Sets have the benefits over classical sets—Rough and Fuzzy Sets. Integrated Fuzzy and Rough Sets work as efficient and intelligent data mining tool [36] and perform much better than individual Rough and Fuzzy Sets to deal with vague information. Idea of crisp equivalence class of RST has been enhanced to generate Fuzzy equivalence class [37] in Fuzzy–Rough Set [38–45] concept. So, each object is represented with membership value having *lower* and *upper approximations* of Fuzzy sets. We partition the objects into H number of Fuzzy clusters [46, 47], F_1, F_2, ..., F_H, representing equivalence classes containing patterns belonging to the class labels. The objects are definitely classified using *lower approximations* of Fuzzy equivalence classes, whereas *upper approximation* of Fuzzy equivalence classes identify the objects which are possibly classified.

Fuzzy–Rough Lower and Upper Approximations
A Fuzzy Set X, describing an output class, is represented by means of Fuzzy partitions [48, 49] comprising *lower* $\underline{P}X$ and *upper approximations* $\bar{P}X$ which are presented in (3.11) and (3.12), respectively.

$$\mu_{\underline{P}X}(F_j) = inf_x\{max(1 - \mu_{F_j}(x), \mu_X(x))\}, \forall j \quad (3.11)$$

$$\mu_{\bar{P}X}(F_j) = sup_x\{min(\mu_{F_j}(x), \mu_X(x))\}, \forall j \quad (3.12)$$

In the above equations, P denotes an attribute subset, $\mu_{F_j}(x)$ and $\mu_X(x)$ stand for membership values of Fuzzy set X for a given object x in F_j, called the Fuzzy equivalence class and X referred to as output class, respectively. Equations (3.13) and (3.14) explicitly represent Fuzzy–Rough *lower* and *upper approximations* [50], respectively.

$$\mu_{\underline{P}X}(x) = sup_{F\in U/R}min(\mu_F(x), inf_{y\in U}max\{1 - \mu_F(y), \mu_X(y)\}) \quad (3.13)$$

$$\mu_{\bar{P}X}(x) = sup_{F\in U/R}min(\mu_F(x), sup_{y\in U}min\{\mu_F(y), \mu_X(y)\}) \quad (3.14)$$

Hereafter, we use the tuple $\langle \underline{P}X, \bar{P}X \rangle$ as a Fuzzy–Rough Set.

Positive Region of Fuzzy–Rough Set
Here, we extend the crisp positive region of traditional RST into Fuzzy positive region. Let an object $x(x \in U)$ lying in the Fuzzy positive region, defined in (3.15).

$$\mu_{POS_P(Q)}(x) = sup_{X\in U/Q}\mu_{\underline{R}X}(x) \quad (3.15)$$

where U/Q denotes partition of objects with respect to attribute set Q.

Dependency of Fuzzy–Rough Set
Dependency of Fuzzy–Rough Set is given using Eq. (3.16).

$$\gamma'_P(Q) = \sum_{x \in U} \mu_{POS_P(Q)}(x)/|U| \qquad\qquad (3.16)$$

3.2.2   Rule-Base

In this section, a new technique of Rough–Fuzzy rule-base generation is proposed. In order to optimize the number of *reducts* and the number of attributes in the *reduct*, Genetic Algorithm, which is widely used for metaheuristic optimization, is utilized for the present application. The algorithm thus used for computing optimal *reducts* is hereafter referred to as Fuzzy–Rough–GA algorithm. The most important aspect of an evolutionary algorithm is the choice of its fitness function. Here, the fitness function is selected in terms of membership values of each object in different classes. The following two fundamental steps are adopted for rule generation in the present context. First, we go for clustering of the data points, disregarding their class labels, although any clustering algorithm would have been employed, we here use Fuzzy C-means clustering algorithm [51] that takes into account of both membership values and distance measures to serve the clustering problem. In the FCM algorithm, we initialize number of clusters equal to the number of classes to check whether the data points falling in a given class are naturally grouped into a cluster. After clustering is over, the attributes of each data point are given a label *high/medium/low* depending on the location of absolute value of the attribute in the dynamic range of the selected attribute. For example, if the attribute value is close enough to the lower bound of the attribute in the entire data set, it is regarded as *low*. On the contrary, if the attribute value falls in the boundary of the high side of the same attribute range in the data set, it is regarded as *high*. In all other cases, attributes are given a label *medium*. Thus, each attribute of the data points are labelled as *high/low/medium*. We can construct the rules based on the labels of the attributes from the data set in the following form.

If x_1 is low, x_2 is high, x_3 is medium,...x_n is high, then class is *J*. Here $x_1, x_2,$ ... x_n are the attributes of the data points; low/medium/high are Fuzzy labels of the attribute, and class *J* is a given class for a selected data point.

The next step in the present context is to use function Mamdani [52]-type reasoning to infer the membership of an object in different classes. The following steps are employed to design FIS using Mamdani-type model.

(i)   Fuzzification of data with respect to each attribute considering its minimum and maximum value.

(ii)   Objects are clustered with fuzzified attribute values where number of clusters is same as the values of different decision attributes.

(iii) Linguistic variables are assigned to each conditional attribute with proper semantic depending on the spread of attribute value for a particular decision attribute value (L).
(iv)   Gaussian membership curves are obtained where parameters are identified by analyzing the patterns of input data set.
(v)   Data elements are sampled randomly to design the rule-base, with membership values of conditional as well as decision attribute values.
(vi)   Subsequent development of the rules, a Fuzzy inference system (FIS), has been constructed employing Mamdani model.
(vii) FIS is applied to obtain belongingness of an object to different classes, used to evaluate Eq. (3.16).

Example 3.1 A data set (Table 3.4) is taken as a try example to explain the proposed Fuzzy–Rough–GA method.

- Lowest and highest ranges of *attr*1 and *attr*2 for spread of respective membership curve are given below:
  *attr*1 = 2–15, *attr*2 = 5–25.
- Sort Table 3.4 according to the decision attribute value (class labels), given in Table 3.5.
- Linguistic variables of different attributes with respect to decision attributes (class labels).
  *attr*1:   lower (2–8), medium (6–12), higher (10–15).
  *attr*2:   too_small (5–16), small (10–20), normal (21–25).
- The membership curves for *attr*1 and *attr*2 are shown in Figs. 3.3 and 3.4, respectively.
- The rule-base considering Table 3.5 is given below:

If *attr*1 is lower and *attr*2 is too_small, then class is 1.
If *attr*1 is lower and *attr*2 is small, then class is 1.
If *attr*1 is lower and *attr*2 is normal, then class is 1.

Table 3.4 Decision system

Samples	attr1	attr2	Class labels
Ob_1	2	10	1
Ob_2	7	5	2
Ob_3	5	15	1
Ob_4	6	8	2
Ob_5	12	16	2
Ob_6	8	20	1
Ob_7	10	25	3
Ob_8	15	22	3
Ob_9	4	17	1
Ob_{10}	13	21	3

Table 3.5 Sorted decision system

Samples	attr1	attr2	Class labels
Ob_1	2	10	1
Ob_2	5	15	1
Ob_3	8	20	1
Ob_4	4	17	1
Ob_5	7	5	2
Ob_6	6	8	2
Ob_7	12	16	2
Ob_8	10	25	3
Ob_9	15	22	3
Ob_{10}	13	21	3

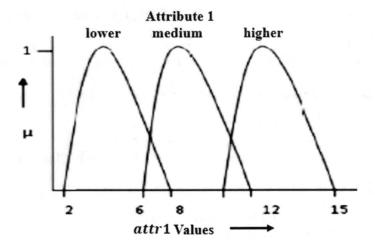

Fig. 3.3 Membership value for $attr1$

If $attr1$ is medium and $attr2$ is small, then class is 1.
If $attr1$ is medium and $attr2$ is normal, then class is 1.
If $attr1$ is lower and $attr2$ is too_small, then class is 2.
If $attr1$ is medium and $attr2$ is too_small, then class is 2.
If $attr1$ is medium and $attr2$ is small, then class is 2.
If $attr1$ is higher and $attr2$ is too_small, then class is 2.
If $attr1$ is higher and $attr2$ is small, then class is 2.
If $attr1$ is medium and $attr2$ is normal, then class is 3.
If $attr1$ is higher and $attr2$ is normal, then class is 3.

Mamdani model [52] has been employed to evaluate the output class membership value.

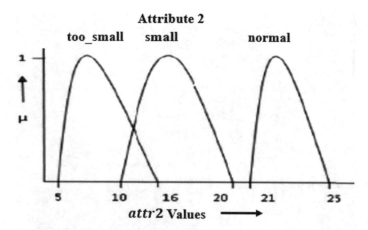

Fig. 3.4 Membership value for *attr*2

3.2.3 Fuzzy–Rough–GA

Before describing the Fuzzy–Rough–GA method, the steps of GA are shown in Fig. 3.5.

The proposed Fuzzy–Rough–GA [53, 54] has been applied to obtain optimum *reduct*, evaluated based on the dependency factor of Fuzzy–Rough Set. At termination, the particular chromosome consisting of the attributes with maximum dependency factor represents the optimum *reduct*.

Chromosomes as population are obtained by sampling attribute values randomly. Each pair of chromosomes is chosen for crossover operation where a crossover point is selected with probability, 0.10. Next, the chromosomes are mutated with a probability less than crossover, say 0.02. The length of chromosomes varies, and different combination of attributes is considered to build new chromosomes in each successive generation. The algorithm terminates when following two conditions are met: (i) The number of generation is higher compared to maximum number of generations (*MAX-NUMBER-OF-GENERATION*) or (ii) there is no change in dependency factor, and the same is higher compared to maximum number of iterations (*MAX-NUMBER-OF-ITERATION*).

3.2.3.1 Crossover Procedure

crossover (x, no.-objs, no.-attrs)

Step 1: Select crossover point in the chromosome randomly.

   crossover probability ← *rand*() % *no.-attrs*

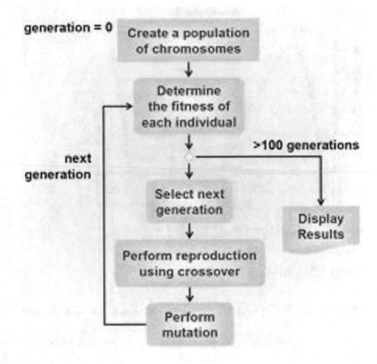

generation = 0

next generation

Fig. 3.5 Steps of genetic algorithm

Step 2: Select one chromosome as Parent1 (*Pr1*) and another chromosome as Parent2 (*Pr2*).

$Pr1 \leftarrow rand() \% \text{ no.-objs}$
$Pr2 \leftarrow rand() \% \text{ no.-objs}$

Step 3: Apply crossover operation of chromosomes to develop new generation.

for ($k = 0$; $k < crossover\ probability$; k ++)

$$t[k] \leftarrow x[Pr1][k]$$
$$x[Pr\ 1][k] \leftarrow x[Pr2][k]$$
$$x[Pr2][k] \leftarrow t[k]$$

3.2.3.2 Mutation Procedure

mutation (x, no.-objs, no.-attrs)
  Step 1: Select the attribute for mutation.

$$mutation\text{-}column \leftarrow rand() \% \, no.\text{-}attrs.$$

  Step 2: Evaluate the attribute which will be mutated.

  (a) for $(j = 0; j < no.\text{-}objs; j++)$

$$mutation\text{-}value \mathrel{+}= x[j][mutation\text{-}column].$$

  (b) Achieve the maximum value from the values of each attribute which are mutated and store in the variable *m*.

  (c) *final-mut-value= (no.-objs * m)/* Final mutation value is calculated.

  Step 3: Updating the mutated attribute

  for $(j=0; j < no.\text{-}objts; j++)$

$$x[j][mutation\text{-}column] \mathrel{+}= mutation\text{-}value.$$

3.2.3.3 Attribute Variation Procedure

variation (coln, no.-w)

Step 1: Evaluate the attributes which are not present in the column-set and keep in the left-set.
Step 2: Obtain a random attribute from the column-set which is replaced by a random attribute of the left-set.

$$Replace\_attr \leftarrow rand(.) \% no.-attrs \, for \, replacing \, using \, column-set$$
$$Selection\_attr \leftarrow rand(.) \% no.-attrs \, from \, left-set \, for \, utilizing \, for \, replacement$$

Step 3: Substitute the respective attribute of column-set by choosing attribute from the left-set.

  For $(i = 0; i < no.\text{-}attrs\text{-}of\text{-}coln\text{-}set; i ++)$
  If $(coln[i] == coln[Replace])$
  $coln[i] = coln[Selection]$

3.2.3.4   GA-Based Dimensionality Reduction Algorithm

ATTRIBUTE-REDUCTION-GA (x)

Input: Membership values of the objects with respect to classes.
Output: Optimum *Reduct* set.

Input: Membership values of the objects with respect to classes.

Output: Optimum *Reduct* set.

Step 1: Initialize $\gamma_{prev} = 0.0$, $\gamma_{best} = 0$, $flg = 0$, *cnt-of-genrn* = 0

Step 2: *Repeat-Until* (*flg* == 1) :

(a) *cnt-of-genrn* += 1

(b) *num-attribute* ← *rand*() % *no.-attributes*

   num-attribute += 1.

(c) Develop the set, named as *Comb* which contains all combinations of *num-attributes*.

(d) Choose an element from *Comb*.

   combination-No.←*rand*() % cardinality of comb set.

(e) Consider the reduced information system *number-attributes* for the combination *combination-num*th .

(f) Get crossover probability.

   If (crossover probability = 0.1)

   Call **crossover (x, no.-objs, no.-attrs)**

(g) Upgrade the Information system (*x*) as needed after crossover.

(h) Determine the probability of mutation

   If (mutation probability = .02)

   Call **mutation (x, no.-objs, no.-attrs)**

(i) Update the Information system (*x*) as needed after execution of mutation.

(j) Call **variation (coln, no.-w)** for getting distinct combination of attributes.

(k) Apply FCM algorithm to determine degree of membership of each object into different cluster.

(l) $\mu_{\underline{P}X}(x) = sup_{F \in U/R} min(\mu_F(x), inf_{y \in U} max\{1 - \mu_F(y), \mu_X(y)\})$

(m) $\mu_{POS_P(Q)}(x) = sup_{X \in U/Q} \mu_{\underline{R}X}(x)$

(n) $\gamma'_P(Q) = \sum_{x \in U} \mu_{POS_P(Q)}(x)/|U|$

(o) if $(\gamma' > \gamma_{prev})$

    Update:

        reduct← current set of attributes.

        $\gamma_{best} = \gamma'$

(p) if $(\gamma_{best} == \gamma_{prev})$

    itr += 1.

(q) Termination condition

    if $((itr == max\text{-}itr\text{-}term) \| (cnt\text{-}of\text{-}gen == max\text{-}gen))$

        Flag = 1.

    end do while

Step 3: Sow the ultimate reduced set of attributes in *Reduct*.

END

3.3 Instance Reduction

For instance reduction, same NSL-KDD data set is considered with 11, 850 instances, and each instance is characterized by 42 attributes. The aim of instance reduction is to eliminate unimportant and redundant instances so that computational complexity of the system is reduced, and classification accuracy is not dominated by the duplicate instances. Simulated Annealing Fuzzy Clustering (SAFC) algorithm [14, 55–57] has been modified using dependency concept of RST to select important and non-redundant instances from NSL-KDD data set.

The SAFC algorithm originally developed to remove shortcomings of Fuzzy *C*-means clustering (FCM) algorithm [58–60]. The proposed algorithm modifies SAFC algorithm by avoiding random perturbation while applied in cluster formation.

The proposed Modified_SAFC algorithm creates clusters considering each attribute. Attribute-dependency concept of RST is applied to select the most significant cluster (MSC) of each attribute, and from each MSC, less important and redundant instances are removed by threshold operation. Most important observation is that classification accuracy does not degrade on removing the redundant instances. This justifies the importance of elimination of the selected redundant attributes.

3.3.1 Simulated Annealing-Based Clustering Algorithm

Kirkpatric et al. [61] proposed a stochastic approach for global optimization, called Simulated Annealing (SA). The SA attempts to find a fair approximation of the global objective function in a large search landscape. The concept of SA is borrowed from metal extraction at high temperature. The metal extraction process includes heating at high temperature for some duration, followed by cooling, so that the system is brought to thermodynamics equilibrium. After the system reaches equilibrium, the object is expected to have many states/configurations in correspondence to a given energy level. Usually, the system is locally distributed around an equilibrium, so that it moves to a new state, having a different energy level. Suppose E_c and E_n, respectively, denote the energy levels at the current and the next state. When $E_c > E_n$, we agree to receive E_n, else probability $\exp\left(-(E_n - E_c)/T\right)$ is considered to accept E_n where T denotes equilibrium temperature. So, when T is large, worse energy level is accepted with higher probability, compared to that of less value of T. Decreasing the temperature gradually and iteratively applying the process, new energy levels are calculated until no more improvements are possible.

Quality of a cluster is measured by compactness [62] within a cluster, while in different clusters, the data points must be well separated. Validity index is used to measure the criterion of clustering. XB validity index [63] for Fuzzy clustering is defined by S in Eq. (3.17).

$$S = \frac{\sum_{j=1}^{c} \sum_{i=1}^{n} \mu_{ij} \left\| x_i - v_j \right\|^2}{n * min_{ij} \left\| x_i - v_j \right\|^2} \tag{3.17}$$

where v_j is the centroid of the clusters, x_i is the data point, and μ_{ij} is the degree of membership value of ith data point belonging to the jth cluster.

In Eq. (3.17), compactness of clusters is denoted by $\frac{\sum_{j=1}^{c} \sum_{i=1}^{n} \mu_{ij} \left\| x_i - v_j \right\|^2}{n}$, which indicates partitioning of the data points.

In the SAFC algorithm [14], Simulated Annealing (SA)-based clustering technique is proposed, where a configuration or state encodes the cluster centers. Due to variable number of clusters, searching of correct value is continued using three functions. Such functions perturb the center, split the center, and delete the center, randomly chosen at each perturbation based on random generation of numbers. The randomness of the algorithm has been removed in the modified SAFC algorithm to generate clusters for each attribute.

3.3.2   Modified_SAFC Algorithm

Flowchart of the Modified_SAFC is presented in Fig. 3.6.

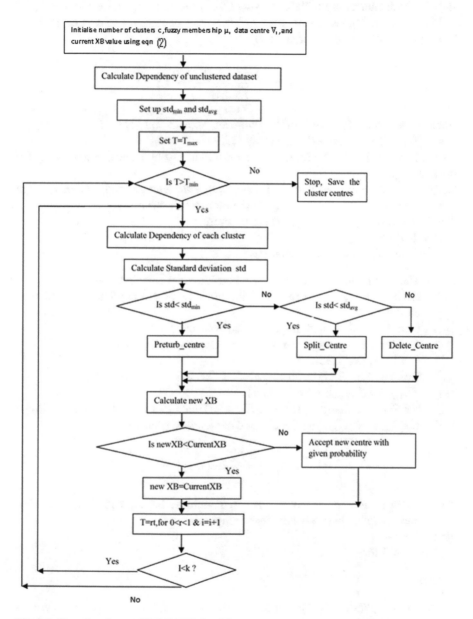

Fig. 3.6 Flowchart for modified SAFC algorithm

Algorithm: *MODIFIED_SAFC* Input: Information Table
  Output: Clusters with XB values in order

Step 1: Number of clusters, say c, is randomly chosen where $c > 1$.
Step 2: The instances are initialized using Fuzzy membership μ_{ij}, where $i = 1 \ldots n$ and $j = 1 \ldots c$ //n denotes no. of data points(n) and c denotes no. of clusters (c).
Step 3: *jth* cluster center v_j for $j = 1$ to c

$$v_j = \frac{\sum_{i=1}^{n}\left(\mu_{ij}\right)^m * x_i}{\sum_{i=1}^{n}\left(\mu_{ij}\right)^m}$$

where m represents fuzzyness of the algorithm, experimentally set as 2 .
Step 4: Calculate current *XB* value using (3.17).
Step 5: Evaluate Eq. (3.5) with respect to individual attribute and define an array for storage.
Step 6: Assume $sd_{min} = m - std$ and $std_{avg} = m + std$ where m and std denote mean and standard deviation, respectively, of the elements in the array.
Step 7: $Tm = max\_Tm$, i.e., highest temperature.
Step 8: If $Tm > min\_Tm$
For $i = 1$ to q//q is number of iterations

  (i)   The data points are clustered based on individual attribute value.
  (ii)   Evaluate Eq. (3.5) for each decision attribute of object with respect to each cluster.
  (iii)   Obtain m and std with respect to each cluster.
  (iv)   If $std < sd_{min}$; *preturb_centre*, else if $std < sd_{avg}$; *split_centre*, Else *delete_centre*.
  (v)   Evaluate Eq. (3.17) to obtain new XB (XB_{new})
  (vi) $XB_{new} < XB_{current}$, center updated.
  (vii)   Set XB_{new} to $XB_{current}$, to restore best XB and updated best centers position.
  (viii) If $XB_{new} > XB_{current}$, accept updated center with probability:

$$\exp\left[\frac{-(XB_{new} - XB_{current})}{T}\right]$$

  (ix)   Assign $Tm = rTm$, where r is a real number between [0,1], representing cooling rate, obviously decreases temperature.
  (ix) $i = i + 1$.
          End-for;

  End.

Current temperature is represented by Tm, whereas max_Tm and min_Tm represent highest and lowest temperatures, respectively. Through experimentations, we determine the parameters. Typical value of maximum temperature is 100, and minimum temperature is 10, where $q = 40$ and $r = 0.9$.

3.3.3 *Most Significant Cluster*

For each attribute, clusters are formed using Modified_SAFC algorithm from which most significant one with respect to each attribute is selected based on highest attribute dependency [64–69]. Based on the concept of Rough Set theory, dependency of individual cluster corresponding to each class label is calculated. Instances in the selected clusters are included as intrusion data set [70]. However, in the worst case, all clusters might be selected; all objects could be included resulting no dimensionality reduction of data. Therefore, the objects, with a certain time of appearance in different clusters, are included in the reduced data set.

Algorithm *reduced_data set*

Input: Clusters for different attributes

Output: Selected objects
Begin

for ($i=1$ to *no._objs*)

Assign initial value of counter, *cntr*[i] ;

for ($j=1$ to *no._attrs*)

{

Step 1: Call Modified_SAFC();

Step 2: Each cluster is evaluated, and we find the one called *MSC* with maximum value. // *MSC* refers most significant cluster.

Step 3: For each object 'i' in MSC, set, *cntr*[i], for the ith object of MSC.

Step 4: Determining Threshold (*Th*)

 Begin

  $S=0$;

  For ($q = 1$ to *no._objs*)

{

$$S = S + cntr[q]$$

}

$$Th = S / no. \_objs$$

End

Step 5: Choosing objects from the corresponding counter

For (j = 1 to *no._objs*)

{

If (*cntr*[j] > *Th*)

j is selected

}

End.

3.4   Results and Discussions

All attributes are not equally important to predict the output. Attributes depending on the respective weightages, they take part in classification and the aim of the work is to find those important attributes, eventually reducing dimensionality of the data set.

3.4.1   Results of Dimension Reduction on Discrete Domain

NSL-KDD intrusion data is invoked for dimension reduction in discrete domain. Discernibility matrix-based dimension reduction technique is applied on discretized network data set, where 200 objects or instances are considered as training data and 100 objects as test data. Reduced dimension set has been achieved and for different classifiers, performance of classification with all attributes and reduced set of attributes is compared (see Tables 3.6 and 3.7).

Table 3.6 Comparison of classifier performance with all attributes and reduced attributes considering tenfold crossvalidation model

Name of classifier	Correctly classified instances (%)		Incorrectly classified instances (%)		Mean absolute error		Root mean squared error		Relative absolute error (%)		Root relative squared error (%)	
	a^*	b^*	a^*	b^*	a^*	b^*	a^*	b^*	a^*	b^*	a^*	b^*
Naïve Bayes	65.6	85.9	34.4	14.0	0.33	0.15	0.56	0.31	112.4	53.1	145.7	82.4
RBF Network	84.7	86.6	15.3	13.3	0.21	0.20	0.33	0.32	73.6	69.8	85.8	83.6
Lazy IB1	95.8	94.0	4.2	5.9	0.04	0.05	0.20	0.24	14.1	20.0	53.1	63.3
PART	97.3	95.7	2.7	4.2	0.03	0.05	0.14	0.17	10.1	19.0	37.1	46.0
NBTree	97.7	95.6	2.2	4.4	0.02	0.05	0.13	0.18	8.1	16.7	34.3	46.5

a^* Set of all attributes, i.e., members of the set = 41
b^* Reduced attribute set, with members = 7

Table 3.7 Comparison of accuracy with all and reduced attributes

Name of classifier		True-positive rate		False-positive rate		Precision		Recall		F-measure	
		a^*	b^*	a^*	b^*	a^*	b^*	a^*	b^*	a^*	b^*
Naïve Bayes	class = 'normal'	0.83	0.56	0.38	0.07	0.32	0.62	0.83	0.56	0.46	0.59
	class = 'anomaly'	0.61	0.92	0.17	0.43	0.94	0.90	0.61	0.92	0.74	0.91
RBF Network	class = 'normal'	0.50	0.57	0.07	0.06	0.59	0.64	0.50	0.57	0.54	0.61
	class = 'anomaly'	0.92	0.93	0.49	0.42	0.89	0.91	0.92	0.93	0.90	0.91
Lazy IB1	class = 'normal'	0.87	0.82	0.02	0.03	0.89	0.85	0.87	0.82	0.88	0.83
	class = 'anomaly'	0.97	0.97	0.13	0.18	0.97	0.96	0.97	0.97	0.97	0.96
PART	class = 'normal'	0.93	0.91	0.01	0.03	0.92	0.86	0.93	0.91	0.93	0.88
	class = 'anomaly'	0.98	0.97	0.06	0.08	0.98	0.98	0.98	0.97	0.98	0.97
NBTree	class = 'normal'	0.94	0.87	0.01	0.02	0.93	0.89	0.94	0.87	0.94	0.88
	class = 'anomaly'	0.98	0.97	0.05	0.13	0.98	0.97	0.98	0.97	0.98	0.97

3.4.2 Confusion Matrix

Information regarding the predicted outcome and original outcome based on a classifier model is presented in the Confusion Matrix [71]. Table 3.8 provides the notion of representation in the confusion matrix

Accuracy (ACC) is defined below.

$$ACC = \frac{p+s}{p+q+r+s}$$

True positive (T − P) is represented below.

$$T - P = \frac{p}{p+q}$$

False positive (F − P) is shown below.

$$F - P = \frac{r}{r+s}$$

True negative (T − N) is presented below.

$$T - N = \frac{s}{r+s}$$

False negative (F − N) is shown below.

$$F - N = \frac{q}{p+q}$$

Precision (P) is presented below.

$$P = \frac{p}{p+r}$$

Network traffic data has been analyzed using SVM classifier with 34 continuous attributes, and confusion matrix is formed as mentioned in Table 3.9 with rate of error 14.04%.

Table 3.8 Confusion matrix representation

		Prediction result		Aggregate
		pos	neg	
Actual value	Pos'	T-P (p)	F-N (q)	POS'
	Neg'	F-P (r)	T-N (s)	NEG'
Aggregate		POS	NEG	

Table 3.9 Values
representing confusion matrix

	Anomaly	Normal	Sum
Anomaly	9399	299	9698
Normal	1365	787	2152
Sum	10,764	1086	11,850

Table 3.10 Values
representing confusion matrix
with less attributes

	Anomaly	Normal	Sum
Anomaly	9395	303	9698
Normal	1442	710	2152
Sum	10,837	1013	11,850

After several iterations, dimensions are reduced, and finally nine important attributes have been selected for classification. Table 3.10 clearly depicts that even though 15 attributes have been reduced, classification accuracy and error rate (currently 14.73%) not affected that much, and therefore, information loss due to dimension reduction is not significant.

3.4.3   Results of Dimension Reduction on Continuous Domain

In order to evaluate accuracy of the proposed DIM-RED-GA() algorithm for dimensionality reduction in continuous domain, following key facts must be observed:

(i)   The extent of dimensionality reduction, i.e., observing the number of attributes present in the *reduct*.
(ii) The accuracy of classification for the *reduct*.

The proposed algorithm is applied to three data sets, and the extent of dimensionality reduction using DIM-RED-GA() and FRQR algorithm is given below (Table 3.11).

Now, the classification accuracy is judged using different classifiers as given in Table 3.12.

Table 3.11 Dimensionality
reduction

Data sets	Actual no. of attributes	DIM-RED-GA
Hypothyroidism	3	3
Pulmonary embolism	4	4
Wine	13	3

Table 3.12 Classification accuracy

Classifier	Hypothyroidism	Pulmonary embolism	Wine
	DIM–RED–GA	DIM–RED–GA	DIM–RED–GA
Bayes net	91:2	71:5	99:43
Naive Bayes	88	75:5	93:82
Naive Bayes updateable	88	75:5	93:82
Logistic	92	75	99:43
Multilayer perceptron	92:4	75	98:31
RBF network (Radial basis function network)	92:4	79	97:19
SMO (Sequential minimal optimization)	88	73	95:50
IBK (Instance-based k nearest neighbor)	87:2	80:5	97:19
K—star	88:4	81:5	97:19
Bagging	96:4	85	99·43
Decision table	92:4	74:5	99:43
J—rip	95:6	80	98:87
NNge	96:4	80:5	99:43
PART	96:8	79:5	98:87
Ridor	96:8	82	98:87
J48	96:4	86:5	98:87
LMT	93:6	85	99:43
NB—tree	97:2	80	99:43
Random forest	96:4	87	99:43
Random tree	87:2	68:5	98:31

3.4.4 Accuracy After Instance Reduction

For instance reduction, initial and final number of clusters and corresponding Davies–Bouldin (DB) validity index [72] is evaluated using SAFC and Modified_SAFC algorithms, applied on NSL-KDD data set, as shown in Table 3.13.

For instance reduction, Modified_SAFC algorithm has been validated on network data set. The number of instances in Most Significant Clusters (MSC) generated using each attribute is given in Table 3.14. The classification accuracy of complete data set is 64.64%. The reduced data set consists of only 7182 objects, and its classification accuracy is 79.88% as shown in Fig. 3.7.

Table 3.13 Comparing results of Modified_SAFC algorithm with SAFC algorithm

Initial number of clusters	Initial DB index	Final number of clusters in modified SAFC algorithm	Final DB index in modified SAFC algorithm	Final number of clusters in SAFC algorithm	DB index in SAFC algorithm
7	0.397	2	0.015	3	0.022
13	2.963	3	0.195	3	0.195
25	8.695	3	0.198	3	0.182
45	304.086	3	0.195	2	0.195
50	876.928	3	3.042	3	3.269

Table 3.14 Number of significant objects for each attributes

Attributes	Final number of clusters	Reduced instances in MSC
1	4	476
2	4	4597
3	6	89
4	3	632
5	6	494
6	2	1974
7	2	5175
8	2	5901
9	2	2705

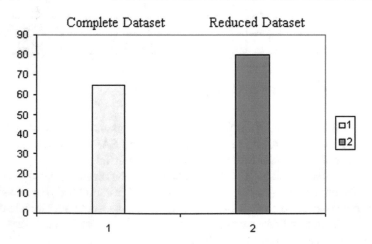

Fig. 3.7 Comparison of classification accuracy of complete data set and reduced data set

3.5 Summary

In the work, dimension reduction for discrete domain using RST has been established with satisfactory outcome. In continuous domain, the limitation of RS attribute reduction method has been discussed, and a novel method DIM-RED-GA using Fuzzy–Rough Sets and GA is proposed. In this approach, the lost information, which is obvious due to discretization, has been recovered using Fuzzy–Rough Sets. DIM-RED-GA, a more informed method, achieves optimal *reduct* set by employing GA, which explores the search space as a stochastic procedure. Stucking at local minima is avoided using Fuzzy–Rough Quick Reduct(FRQR) algorithm. It has been observed that in DIM-RED-GA, the number of attributes in *reduct* is less than those found in other traditional methods without sacrificing accuracy. The bottleneck of Fuzzy–Rough Set–GA-based approach is enormous computational time required for rule generation. It has been observed that when attribute-dependency technique is applied for dimension reduction using support vector machine classifier, the system behaves well with nine continuous attributes where original number of attributes is 34. Computation time has been reduced remarkably with nine continuous attributes. Modificd_SAFC algorithm using RST provides better result compared to SAFC algorithm, while clustering is depicted by DB index value. Modified_SAFC algorithm is used for instance reduction by removing redundant and less informative objects and useful where data set is really high as far as computation time and complexity are concerned. Moreover, comparison of classification accuracy between the complete data set and reduced data set shows that the method is equally good for classification.

References

1. R. Jensen, Q. Shen, *Computational Intelligence and Feature Selection: Rough and Fuzzy Approaches* (Wiley-IEEE Press, 2008)
2. M. Prasad, A. Sowmya, I. Koch, Efficient feature selection based on independent component analysis, in *Proceedings of the 2004 Conference on Intelligent Sensors, Sensor Networks and Information Processing* (2004), pp. 427–432
3. H. Peng, F. Long, C. Ding, Feature selection based on mutual information: criteria of max-dependency, max-relevance, and min-redundancy. IEEE Trans. Pattern Anal. Mach. Intell. **27**, 1226–1238 (2005)
4. Y. Saeys, T. Abeel, Y. Peer, Robust feature selection using ensemble feature selection techniques, in *Proceedings of the European conference on Machine Learning and Knowledge Discovery in Databases—Part II* (Springer, 2008), pp. 313–325. ISBN 978-3-540-87480-5
5. J. Rissanen, Modeling by shortest data description. Automatica **14**, 465–471 (1978)
6. M.H. Hansen, B. Yu, Model selection and the principle of minimum description length. J. Am. Stat. Assoc. **96**, 454 (2001)
7. J.-P. Pellet, A. Elisseeff, Using Markov blankets for causal structure learning. J. Mach. Learn. Res. (2008)
8. J.R. Anaraki, M. Eftekhari, Improving fuzzy-rough quick reduct for feature selection, in *IEEE 19th Iranian Conference on Electrical Engineering (ICEE)* (2011), pp. 1–6
9. E.P. Ephzibah, B. Sarojini, J. Emerald Sheela, A study on the analysis of genetic algorithms with various classification techniques for feature selection. Int. J. Comput. Appl. **8**(8) (2010)

10. S.B. Kotsiantis, D. Kanellopoulos, P.E. Pintelas, Data preprocessing for supervised leaning. Int. J. Comput. Sci. **1**(2) (2006). ISSN 1306-4428
11. X. Zhu, X. Wu, Q. Chen, Eliminating class noise in large datasets, in *Proceedings of the Twentieth International Conference on Machine Learning (ICML-2003)* (Washington DC, 2003)
12. J.M. Hellerstein, *Quantitative Data Cleaning for Large Databases* (United Nations Economic Commission for Europe (UNECE), 2008)
13. B. Zadrozny, Learning and evaluating classifiers under sample selection bias, in *International Conference on Machine Learning ICML'04* (2004)
14. X.Y. Wang, G. Whitwell, J.M. Garibaldi, The application of a simulated annealing fuzzy clustering algorithm for cancer diagnosis, in *Proceedings of IEEE 4th International Conference on Intelligent Systems Design and Application*, Budapest, Hungary, 26–28 Aug. 2004 pp. 467–472
15. K.J. Cios, W. Pedrycz, R. Swiniarski, *Data Mining Methods for Knowledge Discovery* (Kluwer, 1998)
16. A. Skowron, C. Rauszer, The discernibility matrices and functions in information systems, in *Intelligent Decision Support-Handbook of Applications and Advances of the Rough Sets Theory*, ed. by Slowinski (1991), pp. 331–362
17. D. Bhattacharjee, D.K. Basu, M. Nasipuri, M. Kundu, *Reduction of Feature Vectors Using Rough Set Theory for Human Face Recognition*, CoRR, *volume (abs/1005.4044)* (2010)
18. J. Han, R. Sanchez, X.T. Hu, Feature selection based on relative attribute dependency: an experimental study, in *Proceedings of the 10th international conference on Rough Sets, Fuzzy Sets, Data Mining, and Granular Computing—Volume Part I* (2005)
19. Q. Shen, A. Chouchoulas, A rough-fuzzy approach for generating classification rules. Pattern Recogn. **35**, 2425–2438 (2002)
20. Y. Caballero, R. Bello, D. Alvarez, M.M. Garcia, Two new feature selection algorithms with rough sets theory. IFIP AI **209–216**, 2006 (2006)
21. R. Jensen, Combining rough and fuzzy sets for feature selection, Ph.D. thesis (2005)
22. N. Sengupta, Security and privacy at cloud system, in *Cloud Computing for Optimization: Foundations, Applications, and Challenges. Studies in Big Data*, vol 39 ed. by Mishra, B., Das, H., Dehuri, S., Jagadev, A (Springer, Cham, 2018)
23. S. Givant, P. Halmos, *Introduction to Boolean Algebras* (Springer, Berlin, 2009)
24. P.K. Singh, P.S.V.S. Sai Prasad, Scalable quick reduct algorithm: iterative MapReduce approach, in *Proceeding CODS '16 Proceedings of the 3rd IKDD Conference on Data Science*, 2016, Article No. 25 Pune, India—13–16 Mar 2016. (ACM New York, NY, USA ©, 2016)
25. R. Jensen, Q. Shen, Fuzzy-rough sets for descriptive dimensionality reduction, in *Proceedings of the 11th International Conference on Fuzzy Systems* (2002), pp. 29–34
26. F. Abu-Amara, I. Abdel-Qader, Hybrid Mammogram classification using rough set and fuzzy classifier. Int. J. Biomed. Imaging **2009** (2009)
27. M. Yang, S. Chen, X. Yang, A novel approach of rough set-based attribute reduction using fuzzy discernibility matrix, in *Proceedings of the Fourth International Conference on Fuzzy Systems and Knowledge Discovery*, vol. 03 (IEEE Computer Society, 2007), pp. 96–101
28. Neil MacParthalain, Richard Jensen, Measures for unsupervised fuzzy-rough feature selection. Int. J. Hybrid Intell. Syst. **7**(4), 249–259 (2010)
29. A.F. Gomez-Skarmeta, F. Jimenez, J. Ibanez, Data preprocessing in knowledge discovery with fuzzy-evolutionary algorithms, in *IFSA'99, Proceedings of the Eighth International Fuzzy Systems Association World Congress*, vol. I, 17–20 Aug 1999
30. P. Blajdo, J.W. Grzymala-Busse, Z.S. Hippe, M. Knap, T. Mroczek, L. Piatek, A comparison of six approaches to discretization—a rough set perspective, in *Rough Sets and Knowledge Technology*. LNCS, Springer, vol. 5009/2008 (2008), pp. 31–38
31. H. Takahashia, H. Iwakawaa, S. Nakaob, T. Ojiob, R. Morishitab, S. Morikawab, Y. Machidad, C. Machidaa, T. Kobayashia, Knowledge-based fuzzy adaptive resonance theory and its application to the analysis of gene expression in plants. J. Biosci. Bioeng. **106**(6), 587–593 (2008)

32. M. Ektefa, S. Memar, F. Sidi, L.S. Affendey, Intrusion detection using data mining techniques, in *International Conference on Information Retrieval & Knowledge Management* (2010)
33. E. Kesavulu Reddy, V. Naveen Reddy, P. Govinda Rajulu, A study of intrusion detection in data mining, in *Proceedings of the World Congress on Engineering*, vol III, WCE 2011, London, U.K., 6–8 July 2011
34. E. Lughofer, On dynamic soft dimension reduction in evolving fuzzy classifiers, in *Proceedings of the Computational intelligence for Knowledge-Based Systems Design, and 13th International Conference on Information Processing and Management of Uncertainty, IPMU'10* (Springer, Berlin, 2010), pp. 79–88
35. N.J. Pizzi, W. Pedrycz, Classifying high-dimensional patterns using a fuzzy logic discriminant network. Adv. Fuzzy Syst. **2012**, Article ID 920920 (2012), 7 pages
36. O.Z. Maimon, L. Rokach, *Data Mining and Knowledge Discovery Handbook* (Springer, Berlin, 2010)
37. L.A. Zadeh, Fuzzy sets. Inf. Control **8**, 338–353 (1965)
38. R. Roselin, K. Thangavel, C. Velayutham, Fuzzy-rough feature selection for mammogram classification. J. Electron. Sci. Technol. **9**(2) (2011)
39. R.B. Bhatt, M. Gopal, On fuzzy-rough sets approach to feature selection. Elsevier Pattern Recogn. Lett. **26**(7), 965–975 (2005)
40. J. Derrac, C. Cornelis, S. García, F. Herrera, Enhancing evolutionary instance selection algorithms by means of fuzzy rough set based feature selection. Elsevier J. Inf. Sci. **186**, 73–92 (2012)
41. Z. Shaeiri, R. Ghaderi, A. Hojjatoleslami, Fuzzy-rough feature selection and a fuzzy 2-level complementary approach for classification of gene expression data. Sci. Res. Essays **7**(14), 1512–1520 16 Apr 2012
42. P. Kumar, P. Vadakkepat, L.A. Poh, Fuzzy-rough discriminative feature selection and classification algorithm, with application to microarray and image datasets. Appl. Soft Comput. **11**(4), 3429–3440 (2011)
43. R. Jensen, Q. Shen, Semantics-preserving dimensionality reduction: rough and fuzzy-rough-based approaches. IEEE Trans. Knowl. Data Eng. **17**(1) (2005)
44. R. Jensen, Q. Shen, *Rough and Fuzzy Sets for Dimensionality Reduction* (2001)
45. R. Jensen, Q. Shen, New approaches to fuzzy-rough feature selection. IEEE Trans. Fuzzy Syst. **17**(4), 824–838 (2009)
46. A. Banumathi, A. Pethalakshmi, Refinement of K-Means and Fuzzy C-Means. Int. J. Comput. Appl. **39**(17), 11–16 (2012)
47. L. Xie, Y. Wang, L. Chen, G. Yu, An anomaly detection method based on fuzzy C-means clustering algorithm, in *Proceedings of the Second International Symposium on Networking and Network Security (ISNNS '10)* (2010), pp. 089–092
48. J.-H. Man, An improved fuzzy discretization way for decision tables with continuous attributes, in *Proceedings of the Sixth International Conference on Machine Learning and Cybernetics*, Hong Kong, 19–22 Aug 2007
49. N.S. Chaudhari, A. Ghosh, Feature extraction using fuzzy rule based system. Int. J. Comput. Sci. Appl. **5**(3), 1–8 (2008)
50. M. Saha, J. Sil, Dimensionality reduction using genetic algorithm and fuzzy rough concepts, in *2011 World Congress on Information and Communication Technologies* (2011)
51. H. Chih-Cheng, S. Kulkarni, K. Bor-Chen, A new weighted fuzzy C-means clustering algorithm for remotely sensed image classification. IEEE J. Sel. Top. Sig. Process. **5**(3), 543–553 (2011)
52. K. G, Comparison Of Mamdani And Sugeno fuzzy inference system models for resonant frequency calculation of rectangular microstrip antennas. Progr Electromagn. Res B **12**, 81–104 (2009)
53. H. Liu, Z. Xu, A. Abraham, Hybrid fuzzy-genetic algorithm approach for crew grouping, in *Proceedings of the Fifth International Conference on Intelligent Systems Design and Applications (ISDA'05)* (2005), pp. 332–337
54. J.A. Tenreiro Machadoa, A.C. Costa, M. Dulce Quelhas, Entropy analysis of the DNA code dynamics in human chromosomes. Comput. Math. Appl. **62**, 1612–1617 (2011)

55. V. Torra, Fuzzy c-means for fuzzy hierarchical clustering, in *Proceedings of FUZZ '05, the 14th IEEE International Conference On Fuzzy Systems*, 25–25 May 2005. ISBN: 0-7803-9159-4, 646-651

56. S. Bandyopadhyay, *Simulated Annealing for Fuzzy Clustering: Variable Representation, Evolution of the Number of Clusters and Remote Sensing Application*. Machine Intelligence Unit, Indian Statistical Institute (unpublished personal communication) (2003)

57. M.A. Rassam, M.A. Maarof, A. Zainal, Intrusion detection system using unsupervised immune network clustering with reduced features. Int. J. Adv. Soft Comput. Appl. **2**(3) (2010)

58. J.A. Lee, M. Verleysen, Nonlinear projection with the Isotope method, in *ICANN'2002 Proceedings—International Conference on Artificial Neural Networks Madrid (Spain)* ed. by J.R. Dorronsoro. Springer, Lecture Notes in Computer Science 2415, 28–30 Aug 2002, pp. 933–938. ISBN 3-540-44074-7

59. Ch. Aswani Kumar, Reducing data dimensionality using random projections and fuzzy k-means clustering. Int. J. Intell. Comput. Cybern. **4**(3), 353–365 (2011)

60. E. Bingham, H. Mannila, Random projection in dimensionality reduction: applications to image and text data, in *Proceedings of 7th ACM SIGKDD International Conference Knowledge Discovery and Data Mining* (KDD-2001), (San Francisco, CA, 26–29 Aug 2001), pp. 245–250

61. S.C.G. Kirkpatrick, C.D. Gelatt, M. Vecchi, Optimization by simulated annealing. Science **220**(1983), 49–58 (1983)

62. H. Liu, Yu. Lei, Toward integrating feature selection algorithms for classification and clustering. IEEE Trans. Knowl. Data Eng. **17**(4), 491–502 (2005)

63. X.L. Xie, G. Beni, A validity measure for fuzzy clustering. IEEE Trans. Pattern Anal. Mach. Intell. **13**, 841–847 (1991)

64. K. Thangavel, A. Pethalakshmi, Dimensionality reduction based on rough set theory: a review. J. Appl. Soft Comput. **9**(1), 1–12 (2009)

65. M. Sammany, T. Medhat, Dimensionality reduction using rough set approach for two neural networks-based applications, in *Proceedings of the international conference on Rough Sets and Intelligent Systems Paradigms* (Springer, Berlin, 2007), pp. 639–647

66. Q. Shen, A. Chouchoulas, Rough set-based dimensionality reduction for supervised and unsupervised learning. Int. J. Appl. Math. Comput. Sci. **11**(3), 583–601 (2001)

67. J.R. Leathwick, D. Rowe, J. Richardson, J. Elith, T. Hastie, Using multivariate adaptive regression splines to predict the distributions of New Zealand's freshwater diadromous fish. Freshw. Biol. **50**, 2034–2052 (2005)

68. A. Chouchoulas, Q. Shen, Rough set-aided keyword reduction for text categorisation. Appl. Artif. Intell. **15**(9), 843–873 (2001)

69. N. Zhong, J. Dong, S. Ohsuga, Using rough sets with heuristics for feature selection. J. Intell. Inf. Syst. **16**, 199–214 (2001)

70. J.-H. Leet, J.-H. Leet, S.-G. Sohn, J.-H. Ryu, T.-M. Chungt, Effective Value of Decision Tree with KDD 99 Intrusion Detection Datasets for Intrusion Detection System (IEEE, 2008). ISBN: 978-89-5519-136-3

71. N. Sengupta, Intrusion detection system for cloud computing, in Middle East and North Africa Conference for Public Administration Research, Bahrain, 23rd–24th Apr 2014

72. D.L. Davies, D.W. Bouldin, A cluster separation measure. IEEE Trans. Pattern Recogn. Mach. Intell. **1**(2), 224–227 (1979)

Chapter 4
Q-Learning Classifier

Machine learning (ML) is aimed at autonomous extraction of knowledge from raw real-world data or exemplar instances. Machine learning [1] matches the learned pattern with the objects and predicts the outcome. Learning [2] from examples is of three types, supervised, unsupervised [3–7], and reinforcement learning [8–13]. Reinforcement learning works with the combined philosophy of supervised and unsupervised learning, where the machine learns with the help of a critic. Watkins's (1989) Q-learning algorithm is one kind of reinforcement learning method that estimates Q-value by evaluating action-value functions, named as Q-functions. In this chapter, the classical Q-learning algorithm [14, 15] is extended to design and develop an Intrusion Detection System (IDS) [16–20] for real-time [21] applications. Such IDS classifies [22, 23] online NSL-KDD data set accurately either as "*normal*" or "*anomaly*." Hierarchical Reinforcement Learning (HRL) is concerned with structuring of learning behavior based on a prior knowledge. Two-level hierarchical Q-learning [24–26] has been implemented to avoid curse of dimensionality and at the same time to improve the learning speed.

4.1 Q-Learning

Reinforcement learning works on the principle of reward and penalty. Let S_i denote the ith state, a_i the ith action and $Q(s_i, a_j)$ denoting the Q-value while taking action a_j at state s_i. The reward value in RL is estimated, only after the agent reaches its goal. Let $Q(s_i, a_j)$ be a state-action table, such that Q holds the basic primitives of a Markov decision process, i.e.,

$$\sum_{\forall j} Q(s_i, a_j) = 1$$

In other words, the row_sum $= 1$, expressed in Table 4.1.

© Springer Nature Singapore Pte Ltd. 2020
N. Sengupta and J. Sil, *Intrusion Detection*, Cognitive Intelligence and Robotics,
https://doi.org/10.1007/978-981-15-2716-6_4

Table 4.1 Values of Q-table with row_sum = 1

Action → State	a_1	a_2	a_3	a_4
s_1	0.2	0.0	0.5	0.3
s_2	0.3	0.2	0.5	0.0
s_3	0.3	0.4	0.3	0.0

Learning in a Q-Table

During the learning phase, an agent takes an action a_j randomly at state s_i. If after a sequence of actions, it leads to the goal with a success, then all actions taken are rewarded with positive Q-values. However, in the updating process of the Q-table, the row_sum = 1 is always maintained. On the contrary, if the actions selected in sequence leads to a failure to reach the goal, then the corresponding actions at the selected states are penalized with a negative score in Q-values.

The learning process in a Q-table is continued until the Q-values in the table converge. Sample Q-table is shown in Table 4.2. The basic (deterministic) Q-learning Eq. (4.1) is given below.

$$Q(s_i, a) = r(s_i, a) + \gamma * \mathrm{Max}_{a'}\big(Q(s_{i+1}, a')\big) \tag{4.1}$$

where $s_{i+1} = \delta(s_i, a)$; new state (s_{i+1}) is a function $(\delta(.))$ of current state (s_i) and action (a).

Table 4.2 Sample Q-table

Action → State	a_1	a_2	.	.	a_n
s_1	$Q(s_1, a_1)$	$Q(s_1, a_2)$	.....	.....	$Q(s_1, a_n)$
s_2	$Q(s_2, a_1)$	$Q(s_2, a_2)$	.....	.....	$Q(s_2, a_n)$
.	.....	.....	.....	.....	.....
s_n	$Q(s_n, a_1)$	$Q(s_n, a_2)$	.....	.....	$Q(s_n, a_n)$

Fig. 4.1 Block diagram of
Q-learning method

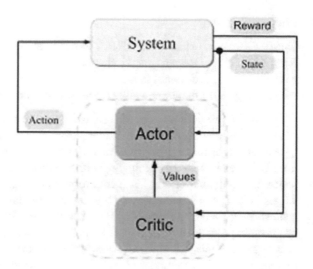

r = reward
γ = discount factor
a' is the highest value of action to change the state from s_i to s_{i+1}.

Planning: In the planning phase, suppose the agent s is at state s_k. It would select an action a_j, such that $Q(s_k, a_j) > Q(s_k, a_\ell)\forall \ell$ in the row. The method of action selection at each state is continued, until the agent reaches the target point.

Diagrammatic representation of Q-Learning is shown in Fig. 4.1.

4.1.1 Extended-Q-Learning Algorithm for Optimized Cut Generation

It is apparent from our background of traditional (deterministic) Q-learning that most efficient actions at a given state usually have high rewards. In other words, the highest reward at a given state determines the next action to be accomplished. The cut generation problem in Rough sets is an important issue as Rough sets require discretized data. The cut generation method returns uniform quantized levels of the attributes based on the measure of their dynamic ranges. The number of quantized levels and the width of the quantized interval, both are important measures for decision making with Rough sets.

In this chapter, we would use extended Q-learning to develop an optimized Q-table of rows, representing cuts and columns representing individual attribute. The choice of intervals is optimized to attain maximum classification accuracy of the proposed Rough set-based classification. Equation (4.2) is applied for extended Q-learning.

$$(s_i, a) = R(s_i, a) + g * \text{Max}(Q(s_{i+1}, a)) \tag{4.2}$$

where

(s_i, a)	value of final Reward matrix element
$R(s_i, a)$	Reward matrix element
g	discount factor
$\text{Max}(Q(s_{i+1}, a))$	maximum value of the actions for next state

Figure 4.2 provides steps of the proposed extended Q-learning.

NSL-KDD data set has been considered for application of the proposed extended-Q-learning algorithm to identify intrusions in real time without any human intervention. Using extended-Q-Learning algorithm, the Intrusion Detection System (IDS) learns optimum cut point for each conditional attribute that discretizes the attribute values in such an effective way so that maximum classification accuracy has been achieved using *reduct* generated by Rough Set theory (RST). The proposed algorithm has been implemented by developing the Reward matrix and Q-matrix in two successive steps. Table 4.3 represents Initialized Reward matrix with p number of rows representing states (p number of cuts for discretization) and q number of columns

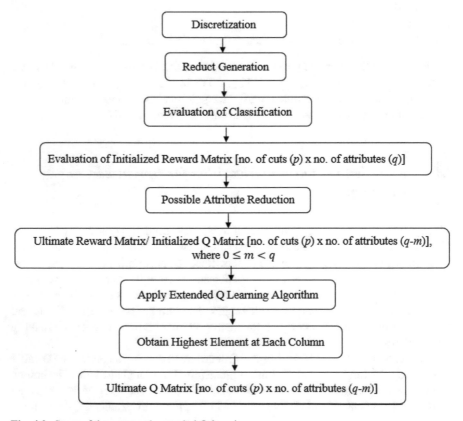

Fig. 4.2   Steps of the proposed extended Q-learning

Table 4.3 Initialized Reward matrix

Attributes ———▶

Number of cuts	a_1	a_2	a_3	.		a_q
d_1	v_{11}	v_{12}	v_{13}	.....	.....	v_{1q}
d_2	v_{21}	v_{22}	v_{23}	.....	.....	v_{2q}
d_3	v_{31}	v_{32}	v_{33}	.....	.....	v_{3q}
.	.....	.....	.....	.....	.....	.....
	.....	.....	.....	.....	.....	.....
d_p	v_{p1}	v_{p2}	v_{p3}	.....	.....	v_{pq}

Table 4.4 Ultimate Reward matrix/Initialized Q-matrix

Attributes ———▶

Number of cuts	a_1	a_2	a_3	.		$a_{(q-m)}$
d_1	v_{11}	v_{12}	v_{13}	.....	.....	$v_{1(q-m)}$
d_2	v_{21}	v_{22}	v_{23}	.....	.....	$v_{2(q-m)}$
d_3	v_{31}	v_{32}	v_{33}	.....	.....	$v_{3(q-m)}$
.	.....	.....	.....	.....	.....	.....
	.....	.....	.....	.....	.....	.....
d_p	v_{p1}	v_{p2}	v_{p3}	.....	.....	$v_{p(q-m)}$

representing attributes of the system. Redundant attributes are reduced from Initialized Reward matrix and Ultimate Reward matrix [no. of cuts (p) × no. of attributes $(q-m)$ where $0 \leq m < q$] is formed which is shown in Table 4.4. Ultimate Reward matrix and Initialized Q-matrix are exactly same from which Ultimate Q-matrix is produced, as shown in Table 4.5.

4.1.1.1 Developing Reward Matrix

The Reward matrix is generated using two steps for applying extended-Q-learning algorithm. In the first step, Initialized Reward matrix and in second step, Ultimate

Table 4.5 Ultimate Q-matrix

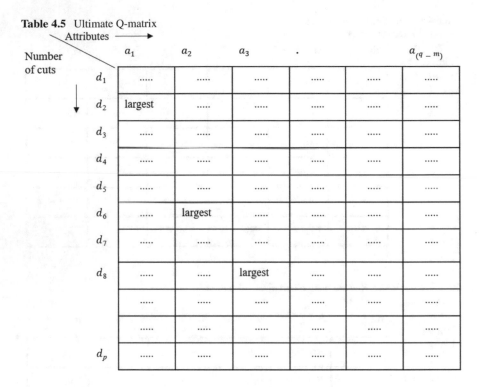

Number of cuts	a_1	a_2	a_3	.		$a_{(q-m)}$
d_1	.....	.....	.....	.....	.....	.....
d_2	largest	.....	.....	.....	.....	.....
d_3	.....	.....	.....	.....	.....	.....
d_4	.....	.....	.....	.....	.....	.....
d_5	.....	.....	.....	.....	.....	.....
d_6	.....	largest	.....	.....	.....	.....
d_7	.....	.....	.....	.....	.....	.....
d_8	.....	.....	largest	.....	.....	.....
	.....	.....	.....	.....	.....	.....
	.....	.....	.....	.....	.....	.....
d_p	.....	.....	.....	.....	.....	.....

Reward matrix have been developed. "Cut" denotes a number which divides the entire range of values of conditional attributes equally. Discretization of conditional attributes of network data set is implemented with the help of these "cut." In the Initialized Reward matrix, rows represent cut and columns represent attribute. In starting row, first value of cut is chosen arbitrarily in the Initialized Reward matrix (M) and finally determined based on designed rule. A number of cuts which are chosen arbitrarily are like 2, 3, 4, etc. Using each cut, say for example, 2, continuous attributes are discretized by dividing the whole span by the cut number, 2. After discretization, *reducts* are generated using discernibility matrix of RST. Based on the values of attributes of *reduct*, classification rules are generated. Classification accuracy is calculated for each *reduct* for the cut 2. For this cut, highest accuracy is noted and the corresponding *reduct* is chosen for selection of attributes in the columns of Initialized Reward matrix (M). Similarly, for all sequential cuts which are in increasing order, classification accuracies are calculated and the corresponding *reduct* for highest accuracy is noted for selection of attributes in the column of Initialized Reward matrix (M). This procedure consisting of these three steps, (i) discretization using cut, (ii) *reduct* generation using discernibility matrix of RST, and (iii) classification accuracy calculation based on the *reduct*, is continued until there is a rise in classification accuracy. In other words, this procedure will be stopped when classification accuracy decreases for two consecutive cuts and the cut for which highest classification accuracy is achieved will be final cut, i.e., number of rows and columns will be decided by using the above procedure. Elements (m_{ij}) of this Initialized Reward matrix (M) will represent classification accuracy for corresponding cut, denoted by i and corresponding attribute(s) of the *reduct* denoted by $j(s)$. For example, if for cut 2, *reduct*, giving highest classification accuracy, consists of attribute 3, 5, 9 of M matrix columns, the values of the M matrix elements, m_{23}, m_{25}, m_{29} will be same. Value of these matrix elements, i.e., values of these classification accuracies, is mapped to the discrete values $[-1, 0, 1]$, using Eq. (4.3).

$$
\begin{aligned}
m_{ij} &= -1; \ if \ accuracy \ of \ red_i < 90\% \\
m_{ij} &= 0; \quad if \ 90\% < accuracy \ of \ red_i < 95\% \\
m_{ij} &= 1; \quad if \ 95\% < accuracy \ of \ red_i < 100\% \\
m_{ij} &= nr; \ if \ attribute j \notin red_i
\end{aligned}
\tag{4.3}
$$

m_{ij} denotes highest accuracy at cut i and for *reduct* red_i where j belongs to the *reduct*, red_i. Equation (4.3) represents that the values of elements of M will be -1 or 0 or 1 if the accuracy is less than 90%, if the accuracy lies between 90 and 95%, if the accuracy is in between 95 and 100%, respectively. It also represents that the values of elements of M will be "nr" if attribute j does not belong to the *reduct*, red_i. Suppose, Initialized Reward matrix consists of 5 columns and attributes in column 1 and in column 5 do not belong to the *reduct* which yields highest accuracy for cut 2, and cut 2 is the first row of the matrix, M. In such case, values of the attributes of column 1 and column 5 will be "nr."

Structure of an Initialized Reward matrix (M) is depicted below.

$$
M = \begin{bmatrix}
nr & -1 & -1 & \ldots & nr \\
nr & 0 & 0 & \ldots & 0 \\
\ldots & \ldots & \ldots & \ldots & \ldots \\
nr & 1 & 1 & \ldots & 1
\end{bmatrix}
$$

In the Initialized Reward matrix (M), it is clear that actions need to be taken only for those attributes which have values other than "nr." Therefore, the attributes for which the value of matrix (M) elements is "nr," can be ignored.

After removing the columns, which have values "nr" for all rows, from the Initialized Reward matrix (M), the Ultimate Reward matrix (URM) is achieved. If at least one attribute in observed as redundant, dimension of URM matrix will be less than the dimension of M. If a specific attribute (say p) does not belong to the *reduct* for a specific cut (say q), then the value of the element (mf_{qp}) is considered as -1 in the matrix URM where this attribute is considered as redundant attribute.

Initialized Reward Matrix (M) Generation Algorithm

Input: A decision table; assume some starting value of cut $= c$
Output: Initialized Reward matrix M $(n \times m)$
Repeat

Step 1: Discretize conditional attributes by applying cut c

Step 2: Develop a set of *reducts* after discretization. A set of *reducts*, say $\left[red_1^c, red_2^c, red_3^c, \ldots, red_q^c\right]$, is generated applying cut c for discretization and *reduct* $\left(red_n^c\right)$ represents nth *reduct* for cut c and number of *reducts* achieved= 1,2,3,....,q

Step 3: Discover red_b^c for which accuracy achieved is highest, i.e., accuracy applying $\left(red_b^c\right) = maximum\left(accuracy\ of\ \left(red_1^c\right),\ accuracy\ of\left(red_2^c\right), \ldots,\ accuracy\ of\ \left(red_q^c\right)\right)$

Step 4: Assign values of the elements of the matrix, M for corresponding cut, c and attributes of *reduct*, red_b^c considering Eq. (4.3)

Step 5: Increase value of cut by 1; $c = c + 1$

Step 6: Until $\left(accuracy\ of\left(red_b^{c-1}\right) = accuracy\ of\left(red_b^{c-2}\right)\right)$ OR $\left(accuracy\ of\left(red_b^{c-2}\right) > accuracy\ of\left(red_b^{c-1}\right) > accuracy\ of\left(red_b^c\right)\right)$.

Ultimate Reward Matrix (URM) Generation Algorithm

Input: Initialized Reward Matrix $M\,(p \times q)$

Output: Ultimate Reward Matrix $URM\,(p \times r)$ where $r <= q$.

Step 1: Check values of the elements of M (m_{xy}) for each column q, are nr

$b = 0$;

    begin

        for $(y= 1$ to $q)$

        Count-for-rows = 0;

    begin

        for $(x=1$ to $p)$

          if $(m_{xy} == nr)$

            Count-for-rows ++;

        end-for

if $(Count\text{-}for\text{-}rows == no.\text{-}of\text{-}cuts)$

    column-to-be-deleted $[b++] = y$; /* b, the index used to keep track of column of Matrix M to be deleted */

end-for

Step 2: Delete $d \in$ *column-to-be-deleted* [ ] /*d is the column for which values of all elements are *nr* and the column to be deleted.

    $r = 0$;

    begin

      for $(y = 1$ to $q)$

      flg-for-deleting-column $= 0$;

    begin

      for $(s = 1$ to $b)$

          if $(t ==$ *column-to-be-deleted* $[s])$

          flg-for-deleting-column $= 1$;

    end-for

      if (*flg-for-deleting-column* $== 0$)

    begin

      for $(x = 1$ to $p)$

         $m_{xr} = m_{xy}$;

    end-for

      $r += 1$;

    end-for

Step 3: Substitute *nr* by -1.

    begin

      for $(x = 1$ to $p)$

        begin

          for $(y = 1$ to $r)$

             if $(m_{xy} ==$ *nr*)

              $m_{xy} = -1$;

        end-for

    end-for.

4.1.1.2   Q-Matrix Development

Q-matrix has been generated in two steps, first Initialized Q-matrix is formed and Ultimate Q-matrix has been evolved from Initialized Q-matrix. The dimension of the Initialized Q-matrix ($Q_{initialized}$) and their representations (state/row is mapped as cut and action/column as conditional attribute) are same to that of the Ultimate Reward matrix (*URM*), developed for a particular data set. In matrix $Q_{initialized}$, all the values of elements of last row are ones, where this last row is mapped with Goal state referring maximum classification accuracy and values of rest of the elements of matrix, $Q_{initialized}$, are zeroes. The Goal state with highest classification accuracy is attained through training. Learning procedure, consisting of some occurrences, continues till Goal state is achieved, i.e., values of all elements of extended Q-matrix exceed the value "0" referring the classification accuracy lying within acceptable range which is more than 90%. The modified Q-matrix is named as Ultimate Q-matrix or $Q_{ultimate}$.

Extended-Q-Learning Algorithm

BEGIN

Input: Ultimate Reward Matrix, *URM* $(p \times r)$

Output: the Ultimate Q-Matrix, $Q_{ultimate}$ $(p \times r)$

Step 1: Assign values of all elements of $Q_{initialized}$ and $Q_{ultimate}$ $(p \times r)$ equal to '0'.

Step 2: Consider the $s_p = s_{goal}$ of $Q_{ultimate}$ to 1.

   for $(y = 1 \ .... \ r)$

   $Q_{ultimate}$ $[p]$ $[y] = 1$;

   end.

Step 3: Obtain *SM* $(r \times 3)$ from *URM* $(p \times r)$ assigning 0 / 1 to the corresponding elements of *URM*. // *SM*, a sparse matrix

Step 4: Mark that i $(i = 1....n)$ having *no-action*

   no-action-size = 0;

   begin

     for $(i = 1$ to $n)$

     flag2 = 0;

   begin

     for $(j = 1$ to $p)$

if $(URM [i] [j] \geq 0)$

   $flag2 = 1;$

end-for

   if $(flag2 == 0)$

   no-*action* [*no-action-size* ++] = *i* ;

end-for.

Step 5: Initialize the *flag* [ ] to 0.

Step 6: Starting of episodes

   begin

      do while

      count = 0;

/*Start operation from *i*=0 (i.e., Start state) and continue until *i*=*n* (i.e., Goal State) is attained */

   begin

      while $(SM [count] [0] ! = (n-1))$

         state = *SM* [*count*] [0] ;

      begin

   if $((SM [count] [2] == 0)$ and $(flag [state] == 0))$

   action-number = *SM* [*count*] [1] ;

   Calculate MAX $[Q_{ultimate} (next\text{-}state, all\text{-}actions)]$

   Update the *Q*-Matrix

   $Q_{ultimate} [state][action\text{-}number] = (URM[state][action\text{-}number] + (g * MAX));$

      Update *SM* $(r \times 3)$

      Reinitialize the *flag* [ ] to 0.

/* Checking all values of $Q_{ultimate}$ [ ][ ] has been updated */

   flag-end = 0 ;

   begin

      for $(k = 1$ to $a)$

      if $(SM [k] [2] == 0)$

      flag-end = 1 ;

   end-for

   End do while $(flag\text{-}end == 1)$;

END.

Thus, Ultimate Q-matrix $(Q_{ultimate})$ has been obtained where for each column q, the highest value of the elements, m_{pq} is noted. The value of the element m_{pq} represents the optimum cut, p for discretization of a particular continuous attribute, q, which results in highest classification accuracy. Considering the decision Table 4.6, Initialized Reward matrix (M), Ultimate Reward matrix (URM), and Ultimate Q-matrix ($Q_{ultimate}$) are depicted below.

$$M = \begin{array}{c} \\ State\ 0 - Cut4 \\ State\ 1 - Cut5 \\ State\ 2 - Cut6 \\ State\ 3 - Cut7 \\ State\ 4 - Cut8 \end{array} \begin{array}{cccccc} CA_1 & CA_2 & CA_3 & CA_4 & CA_5 & CA_6 \\ \begin{bmatrix} nr & -1 & -1 & nr & nr & nr \\ nr & nr & 0 & 0 & nr & nr \\ nr & 0 & 0 & 0 & nr & nr \\ nr & nr & 1 & 1 & nr & nr \\ nr & 1 & 1 & 1 & nr & nr \end{bmatrix} \end{array}$$

Actions (Attributes)

Initialized Reward Matrix, M

Actions (Attributes)

$$URM = \begin{array}{c} \\ State\ 0 - Cut4 \\ State\ 1 - Cut5 \\ State\ 2 - Cut6 \\ State\ 3 - Cut7 \\ State\ 4 - Cut8 \end{array} \begin{array}{ccc} CA_2 & CA_3 & CA_4 \\ \begin{bmatrix} -1 & -1 & -1 \\ -1 & 0 & 0 \\ 0 & 0 & 0 \\ -1 & 1 & 1 \\ 1 & 1 & 1 \end{bmatrix} \end{array}$$

Ultimate Reward Matrix, URM

Table 4.6 Partial data set of NSL-KDD

Objects	CA_1	CA_2	CA_3	CA_4	CA_5	CA_6	Decision class
OB_1	13	118	2425	1	1	26	1
OB_2	0	44	0	4	3	255	1
OB_3	0	0	44	1	1	255	1
OB_4	0	53	55	511	511	255	2
OB_5	0	0	0	1	1	16	1
OB_6	0	54540	8314	2	9	255	1
OB_7	0	0	0	228	9	255	1
OB_8	7570	0	44	1	1	255	1
OB_9	0	56	52	294	294	255	2
OB_{10}	0	192	0	2	2	93	2

$$
Q_{initialized} = \begin{matrix} & CA_2 & CA_3 & CA_4 \\ State\ 0 - Cut4 \\ State\ 1 - Cut5 \\ State\ 2 - Cut6 \\ State\ 3 - Cut7 \\ State\ 4 - Cut8 \end{matrix} \begin{bmatrix} 0 & 0 & 0 \\ 0 & 0 & 0 \\ 0 & 0 & 0 \\ 0 & 0 & 0 \\ 1 & 1 & 1 \end{bmatrix}
$$

Actions (Attributes)

Initialized Q matrix, $Q_{initialized}$

$$
Q_{ultimate} = \begin{matrix} & CA_2 & CA_3 & CA_4 \\ State\ 0 - Cut4 \\ State\ 1 - Cut5 \\ State\ 2 - Cut6 \\ State\ 3 - Cut7 \\ State\ 4 - Cut8 \end{matrix} \begin{bmatrix} 1.00 & 0.8 & 1 \\ 1.64 & 1 & 1.44 \\ 0.8 & 1.8 & 1.64 \\ 1.44 & 1.8 & 1.8 \\ 1 & 1 & 1 \end{bmatrix}
$$

Actions (Attributes)

Ultimate Q matrix, $Q_{ultimate}$

It is observed in $Q_{ultimate}$ that the highest value in the first column is at row 2, which represents that for the attribute CA_2 (represented by the first column), optimum cut is 5 (represented by the second row). Therefore, from Ultimate Q-matrix, it is derived that if cut 5 is applied for discretization of continuous attribute CA_2, highest classification accuracy is achieved for intrusion detection.

4.2 Hierarchical-Q-Learning Approach

The flat structure reinforcement learning (Q-Learning) algorithm suffers from increased computational complexity when the number of state variables increases in the problem domain. Hierarchical Reinforcement Learning is designed to deal with such problems. Hierarchical Reinforcement Learning is based on semi-Markov decision process (SMDP) [27], extended form of the traditional Markov decision process [27].

In Hierarchical-Q-Learning [28, 29], the whole problem is divided into sub-tasks and is assigned to different hierarchical levels to avoid the consequence of the curse of dimensionality. Order of execution of each sub-task depends on the requirement of the system. Reward of each sub-task in any of the hierarchical level contributes toward the total reward of learning. Terminating condition of each sub-task forms the goal of learning. Hierarchical-Q-Learning algorithm has been modified and applied in the book to obtain optimized variation in the range of linguistic labels of the Fuzzy rules. The rule-based classifier is built using the rules that maximize the accuracy of classification in detecting intrusions.

4.2.1   Definition of Semi-Markov Decision Process (SMDP)

An SMDP is defined as MD $= \langle$F, C, S, R, N$\rangle$, where F represents a finite set of states, C denotes a finite set of actions, and the transition probability function, S, is defined as S: F $\times$ C $\times$ F$'$ $\times$ M $\rightarrow$ [0, 1].

The transition probability function, defined as S(F$'$, M$|_{F, C}$), is the probability of transitioning state F to state F$'$ in M time steps, where C is the action taken.

The reward function, D, is defined as D: F $\times$ C $\times$ F$'$ $\rightarrow$ D. The reward function defines the reward for moving from state F to state F$'$ by performing action C.

The transition time function, N, is defined as N: F $\times$ C $\times$ F$'$ $\rightarrow$ M. The transition time function N(F$'$$|_{F, C}$) is the completion time for taking action C in state F to reach F$'$.

A policy ρ is a function, defined as ρ: F $\rightarrow$ C, denotes an action C is taken by the agent in a given state F.

4.2.2   Optimization of Linguistic Labels

Fuzzy–Rough Set theory and Genetic Algorithm (GA) have been applied in Chap. 3 of the book to reduce dimensionality of continuous data set and selecting optimum reducts [30–33]. To classify the data, Fuzzy rule set is derived where antecedents are mapped as attributes or set of attributes (*reduct*) with different linguistic variables or labels. Range of different linguistic labels corresponding to each Fuzzy variable is initialized by analyzing the data set. Then different variation to the range of the labels is generated using standard deviation of each attribute. The proposed Hierarchical-Q-Learning algorithm has been verified by applying to Wine data set, where two levels are considered as level_1 and level_2. In level_1 *reduct*s are considered, while in level_2, individual attributes are considered for optimizing linguistic labels assigned to them. The performance of the classifier is evaluated before and after learning, demonstrating improvement in classification accuracy by imparting training using Hierarchical method.

4.2.2.1   Data Preparation

Data preparation comprises two main steps. First, initial assignment of range of linguistic labels to each attribute is performed. Second, the variation of range is evaluated by applying Hierarchical-Q-Learning algorithm to learn optimum range of linguistic labels.

Initial Assignment of Range

Following steps are performed for initial assignment of range to linguistic labels.

(i)   The training data set is arranged according to their class labels.

(ii) For each attribute corresponding to a particular class label, the minimum and maximum attribute values are noted to determine the range.

(iii) A linguistic label is assigned to each range of every attribute.

Variation of Range

To evaluate the variation of range of different linguistic labels for Fuzzy rule set, the following steps are undertaken. The rule set is used as dimension of the Initialized Q-Matrix.

(i) First standard deviation (sd_total) of the whole data set and the same for each of the conditional attributes (sd_attr) are calculated.

(ii) Next, for n number of conditional attributes, *mean* of standard deviations of each attribute (sd_attr) is calculated.

(iii) The deviation (dev) between sd_total and sd_attr is also evaluated.

The sd_attr is considered as the starting variation. The other variations are obtained using Eq. (4.4).

$$var_{i+1} = sd_{attr} + (i * dev) \qquad (4.4)$$

where $i = 1, 2,..., n$.

4.2.2.2 Proposed Hierarchical-Q-Learning Algorithm

Consider a problem with two hierarchical levels denoted by level_1 and level_2. We require to learn the optimum linguistic labels in the rule set by applying the proposed Hierarchical-Q-Learning algorithm. These two levels are executed sequentially, considering *reduct* in level_1 and individual attribute in level_2.

Developing Hierarchical Reward Matrix

The Reward matrix is generated in two steps in the proposed algorithm. In the first step, Initialized Reward matrix is developed, and in second step, Ultimate Reward Matrix is developed. In level_1, each variation is mapped to a row (i.e., the state) and each *reduct* to a column (i.e., the action). Classification rules are developed based on individual *reducts* and applying the rule-based classifier, classification accuracy is derived for each particular *reduct*. Values of elements of Initialized Reward matrix represent the classification accuracy for a particular cut and *reduct*. To form the Initialized Reward matrix, accuracy values are discretized to $[-1, 0, 1]$ depending on the range of continuous values of classification accuracy as expressed in (4.5). Next, the result of level_1 is utilized to form the Initialized Reward matrix of level_2 of the proposed Hierarchical-Q-Learning algorithm. In level_2, the optimized variation of each *reduct* (as calculated from level_1) is considered as states and the attributes as actions. The Initialized Reward matrix is formed in the same way as in level_1.

$$r_{ij} = -1; \quad if \; accuracy \; of \; Red_i < 65\% \; OR \; if \, attribute \, j \notin Red_i$$
$$r_{ij} = 0; \quad if \; 65\% < accuracy \; of \; Red_i < 75\% \tag{4.5}$$
$$r_{ij} = 1; \quad if \; 75\% < accuracy \; of \; Red_i < 100\%$$

where selected *attribute j* in *reduct* set Red_i yields maximum accuracy at *cut i*.

The logic of developing Initiailized Reward matrix and Ultimate Reward matrix [14] in the proposed Hierarchical-Q-Learning algorithm is similar to that of the extended-Q-learning algorithm, and thus, the same is omitted to avoid repetition.

Developing Hierarchical Q-Matrix

Hierarchical Q-matrix (HQ) has been evolved from the Ultimate Reward matrix. The Start state of the HQ matrix corresponds to a particular range of linguistic label, and the Final state or Goal state is represented as the state where highest classification accuracy is achieved. Initially, values of the elements of each row except the last row of the HQ matrix are zeroes. The values of all elements of last row, corresponding to the Goal state, are ones exhibiting highest classification accuracy. Learning algorithm, with some occurrences, continues till Goal state is achieved, i.e., values of all elements of HQ matrix exceed the value "0" referring the classification accuracy lying within acceptable range. At the end of learning, optimal range of values to linguistic labels is obtained at the Goal state.

The logic of developing Initialized HQ matrix and Ultimate HQ matrix is same to that of extended-Q-learning algorithm, and so is omitted to avoid repetition. Therefore, the HQ matrix is developed where for each column j, the highest value of the element, hq_{ij} is noted, denoting the optimum variation value, i, for *reduct Red_j*. After evaluation of the HQ matrix, the optimized range of values of linguistic labels is utilized to obtain optimized range of variation to the linguistic labels of each attributes in level_2, following the same procedures. The optimized range of values of linguistic labels is utilized to design the Fuzzy rule set. Finally, a rule-base classifier is built and evaluated using the test data set to measure the performance of the classifier.

4.3 Results and Comparisons

In the work, NSL-KDD data set [34] is used for learning the environment with 34 continuous and 7 discrete attributes. Results are shown in two parts, first part is for extended-Q-learning and the second part is for hierarchical-Q-Learning algorithms.

4.3.1 Result of Extended-Q-Learning Algorithm

At the beginning of extended-Q-learning algorithm, discretization of all conditional continuous attributes is performed by applying same cut value and accordingly *reducts* are formed. For example, from NSL-KDD data set, 200 objects are considered as training data set. As 34 continuous attributes are there in the data set, discretization is applied using cut 2 and number of *reducts* developed is 4. Using these four *reducts*, classification accuracy is calculated for test data set considering 100 objects from NSL-KDD data set. Result of classification accuracy corresponding to these four *reducts* using cut 2 is presented in the following table.

From Table 4.7, it is clear that values of classification accuracy for all *reducts* are same. In such case, attributes for any *reduct* can be selected as columns for forming the Initialized Reward matrix. Here, in this case, *reduct* R_0 is selected, i.e., attributes 2, 31, 32, and 34 are chosen to form the Initialized Reward matrix.

The procedure is repeated by applying discretization on all continuous attributes using cut 3, 4, 5, 6, 7, 8, 9, and corresponding *reducts* are generated. The attributes belonging to the *reducts* for each cut, providing maximum classification accuracy, are chosen as columns for forming the Initialized Reward matrix. Values of classification accuracies for corresponding cuts are presented graphically in Fig. 4.3 and are represented in textual form in Table 4.8. It is clear to note that the values of classification accuracies are monotonically decreasing from cut 9, i.e., classification accuracy for cut 10 is less than that of cut 9 and classification accuracy for cut 11 is less that of cut 10. Therefore, the Goal state is achieved at cut 9 which indicates the number of rows of Initialized Reward matrix will be 8, starting from cut 2 and ending at cut 9.

Another result is shown in Fig. 4.4 using second data set given in Table 4.9.

Table 4.7 Classification accuracy for four *reducts*

Reduct	Attributes	Classification accuracy (%)
R_0	34,32,2,31	90.7
R_1	34,32,2,33	90.7
R_2	9,32,2,31	90.7
R_3	9,32,2,33	90.7

Fig. 4.3 Cut versus accuracy for first data set given in Table 4.8

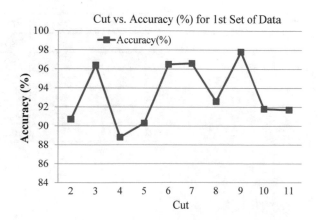

Table 4.8 Classification accuracy for different cuts for first set of data

Cut	Classification accuracy (%)
2	90.7
3	96.4
4	88.8
5	90.3
6	96.5
7	96.6
8	92.6
9	97.8
10	91.8
11	91.7

Fig. 4.4 Cut versus accuracy for second data set given in Table 4.9

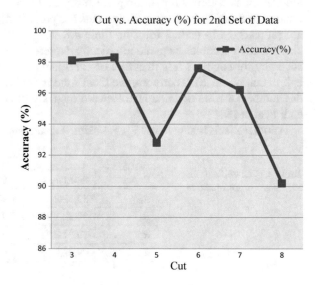

Table 4.9 Cut versus accuracy for second set of data

Cut	Accuracy (%)
3	98.11
4	98.3
5	92.8
6	97.6
7	96.2
8	90.2

Finally, Ultimate Reward matrix will be formed with 11 columns representing attributes 4, 5, 9, 22, 28, 29, 31, 32, 33, 35 and with 8 rows representing cut 2, 3, 4, 5, 6, 7, 8, 9, as shown in Table 4.10. Therefore, the Ultimate Reward matrix has 8 rows and 11 columns. The Ultimate Q-matrix is achieved by implementing extended-Q-learning algorithm, depicted in Table 4.11. Therefore, Ultimate Q-matrix and optimum cuts for discretization of different continuous attributes are acquired where these attributes, belonging to different *reducts*, produce maximum classification accuracy. It is interestingly noted that if cut 4 is considered to discretize the continuous attribute 4, cut 6 is applied for discretization of continuous attribute 5, and so on and the derived *reduct* is applied for classification on test data set, and a classification accuracy of 98.2% is obtained in detecting intrusions.

4.3.2 Experiments Using Synthetic Data Set

Network data is synthetically generated to verify the extended-Q-learning algorithm in detecting intrusions as "*anamoly*" or "*normal.*" Correlation between training and synthetically generated test data set are studied by evaluating Pearson's correlation coefficient (r) [35], defined below.

$$r = \frac{m \Sigma pq - (\Sigma \mathrm{p})(\Sigma \mathrm{q})}{\sqrt{(m(\Sigma p^2) - (\Sigma \mathrm{p})^2)}\sqrt{(m(\Sigma q^2) - (\Sigma q)^2)}}$$

where the number of specimens is represented by m, and two variables are p and q. Range of value of r is from -1 to $+1$. Value of Pearson's correlation coefficient expresses correlation between two variables. The value of r is close to $+1$ which represents that both variables (p and q) have a strong positive linear correlation, value of r is near to 0 which denotes that both variables (p and q) have no correlation, and r is near to -1 which expresses that both variables (p and q) have a strong negative correlation. Synthetic data sets are generated, out of which some have strong positive, strong negative, and no correlationship with the training data set. For detecting intrusions, classification accuracies are calculated using proposed method for those synthetic data set as real-time objects. Classification accuracy of synthetic data set and correlation between synthetic data sets and training data sets are presented in Table 4.12. It is noted that classification accuracy is decreased as the correlation between synthetic data set and training data set closes to zero.

Table 4.10 Ultimate Reward matrix using part of NSL-KDD data set

Cut	Attribute number (A)										
	4	5	9	22	28	29	31	32	33	34	35
2	−1	−1	−1	−1	−1	−1	0	0	−1	0	−1
3	−1	−1	−1	−1	−1	−1	−1	−1	−1	−1	−1
4	−1	−1	−1	−1	−1	−1	−1	0	−1	−1	−1
5	−1	−1	0	−1	−1	−1	−1	0	0	−1	−1
6	−1	−1	−1	−1	−1	−1	−1	−1	−1	−1	−1
7	−1	−1	−1	−1	−1	−1	−1	−1	−1	−1	−1
8	−1	−1	−1	−1	−1	−1	0	−1	−1	−1	−1
9	1	−1	−1	1	1	−1	1	−1	−1	−1	−1

Table 4.11 Ultimate Q-matrix from Ultimate Reward matrix of Table 4.10

Cut	Attribute number (A)										
	4	5	9	22	28	29	31	32	33	34	35
2	0	0	0	0	0	0	0.8	0.8	0	0.8	0
3	0	0	1	1	0	1	0	0	0	0	1
4	0	0	0	0	0	0	0	0	0	0	0
5	0	0	0.8	0	0	0	0	1.44	1.85	0	0
6	0	1	0	1.8	2.312	0	2.312	0	0	0	0
7	0	0	0	1	0	1.64	1.64	0	0	0	0
8	0	0	0	0	0	0	0.8	0	0	0	0
9	1	−1	−1	1	1	−1	1	−1	−1	−1	−1

Table 4.12 Accuracy using synthetic data and correlation between synthetic and training data

Synthetic data set	Correlation	Accuracy (%)
1	−0.1376	96.86
2	−0.0072	95.44
3	0.0058	87.98
4	0.0079	88.98
5	1	95.13

Table 4.13 *Reduct* set with attributes

Reduct	Attributes
R_1	6, 11, 12
R_2	6, 10, 11, 12
R_3	4, 5, 6, 12
R_4	2, 6, 10, 12
R_5	5, 6, 10, 11, 12
R_6	4, 6, 10, 11, 12
R_7	1, 5, 6, 11, 12
R_8	5, 6, 9, 10, 11, 12

4.3.3   Results of the Proposed Hierarchical-Q-Learning Algorithm

In the work, the proposed hierarchical-Q-learning algorithm is applied on the Wine data set with 13 conditional attributes. The *reduct* set is evaluated, as indicated in Table 4.13. Then, the variation is calculated using expression (4.4), as mentioned in Table 4.14.

Table 4.14 Variation with value

Variation	Values
Var0	0
Var1	0.20610
Var2	0.22830
Var3	0.25041
Var4	0.27252
Var5	0.29463
Var6	0.31674
Var7	0.33885
Var8	0.36096

In level_1 of the proposed hierarchical-Q-learning algorithm, optimized variations are applied to each of the *reducts*. The Initialized Reward matrix and Ultimate Reward matrix are presented in Tables 4.15 and 4.16, respectively.

The Ultimate Reward matrix is same as the Initialized Reward matrix, since there is no column consisting of all -1's in the corresponding rows.

Now maximizing the goal of each row of Ultimate HQ matrix, the variation is obtained and applied to each of the *reduct*, as shown in Table 4.17 which has been utilized to proceed to level_2.

Level_2 optimizes the variation when applied to each of the attributes. The variations along with the best *reduct* found in level_1 are considered as the states and the attributes on which variations are applied as actions. The evaluation result of Initialized Reward matrix, Ultimate Reward matrix, and Ultimate HQ matrix are presented in Tables 4.18, 4.19, and 4.20 respectively.

Table 4.15 Initialized Reward matrix in level_1

Variation	Reducts (R_i)							
	R_1	R_2	R_3	R_4	R_5	R_6	R_7	R_8
Var0	+1	+1	0	+1	+1	0	+1	0
Var1	+1	+1	+1	+1	+1	+1	0	0
Var2	+1	+1	+1	+1	+1	+1	0	0
Var3	+1	0	+1	−1	0	0	0	0
Var4	+1	0	+1	−1	0	0	0	0
Var5	+1	0	+1	−1	0	0	0	0
Var6	+1	0	+1	−1	0	0	0	0
Var7	+1	0	+1	−1	0	0	0	0
Var8	+1	+1	+1	0	0	+1	0	0

Table 4.16 Ultimate Reward matrix in level_1

Variation	Reducts (R_i)							
	R_1	R_2	R_3	R_4	R_5	R_6	R_7	R_8
Var0	1.0	1.8	1.44	2.952	2.952	2.361	3.3616	2.3616
Var1	1.0	1.8	2.44	2.44	2.952	2.952	1.952	1.952
Var2	1.0	1.8	1.8	2.44	2.44	2.44	1.44	1.44
Var3	1.0	0.8	1.8	0.0	1.44	1.44	1.44	1.44
Var4	1.0	0.8	1.8	0.0	1.7216	1.7216	1.7216	1.7216
Var5	1.0	0.8	2.152	0.0	1.952	1.952	1.952	1.952
Var6	1.0	1.44	2.44	0.0	1.44	1.44	1.44	1.44
Var7	1.8	0.8	1.8	0.0	0.8	0.8	0.8	0.8
Var8	1.0	1.0	1.0	0.0	1.0	1.0	0.0	0.0

Table 4.17 Optimal
variation for *Reduct*

Variation	*Reduct*
Var0	R_7
Var1	R_5
Var2	R_4
Var3	R_3
Var4	R_3
Var5	R_3
Var6	R_3
Var7	R_1
Var8	R_6

Now, the Ultimate Reward matrix is formed as presented in Table 4.19, by eliminating the column from Table 4.18 which has all its elements as −1.

Now maximizing the goal of each column of the Ultimate HQ matrix, the variation is obtained for each of the attribute in order to improve the accuracy of classification. This is shown in Table 4.21.

A comparative study of classification accuracy (a) before learning and (b) after learning with (c) no-variation and (d) the optimized range of variation to the linguistic labels of each attributes is evaluated, showing improvement in performance, shown in Table 4.22.

4.4   Summary

Extended-Q-learning algorithm and *RST* have been applied for development of online IDS which detect intrusion having accuracy of 98%. The environment is learned with reduced dimension and selected features to achieve the Goal state [36–38]. In this book, different methods of discretization for cut generation, attribute selection, and calculation of classification accuracy are manipulated concurrently to optimize the cost of computation. It is noted that if same cut is applied for discretization of all continuous attributes of the decision system, classification accuracy varies in a large way even for two successive values of cut. By implementing extended-Q-learning algorithm, it has been observed that if an optimum cut is applied for discretization of a particular continuous attribute, highest classification is achieved. The proposed method is established through testing with different data sets for online intrusion detection revealing recommendable classification accuracy.

In this work, concept of hierarchical Q-learning has been highlighted, and the concept is utilized to propose an algorithm that is implemented in two levels. There are many advantages in Hierarchical Reinforcement Learning. First, as number of variables is reduced in each hierarchical level, learning can be faster as few trials are needed. Second, learning for any sub-task, in any level of hierarchy can be

Table 4.18 Initialized Reward matrix in level_2

Reduct with variation	Attribute number ($Attr_s$)												
	$s = 0$	$s = 1$	$s = 2$	$s = 3$	$s = 4$	$s = 5$	$s = 6$	$s = 7$	$s = 8$	$s = 9$	$s = 10$	$s = 11$	$s = 12$
Var0-R_7	−1	+1	−1	−1	−1	+1	+1	−1	−1	−1	−1	+1	+1
Var1-R_5	−1	−1	−1	−1	−1	+1	+1	−1	−1	−1	+1	+1	+1
Var2-R_4	−1	−1	+1	−1	−1	+1	+1	−1	−1	−1	+1	−1	+1
Var3-R_3	−1	−1	−1	−1	+1	+1	+1	−1	−1	−1	−1	−1	+1
Var4-R_3	−1	−1	−1	−1	+1	+1	+1	−1	−1	−1	−1	−1	+1
Var5-R_3	−1	−1	−1	−1	+1	+1	+1	−1	−1	−1	−1	−1	+1
Var6-R_3	−1	−1	−1	−1	+1	−1	+1	−1	−1	−1	−1	−1	+1
Var7-R_1	−1	−1	−1	−1	−1	−1	+1	−1	−1	−1	−1	+1	+1
Var8-R_6	−1	−1	−1	−1	−1	−1	+1	−1		−1	+1	+1	+1

Table 4.19 Ultimate Reward matrix in level_2

Reduct with variation	Attribute number ($Attr_s$)							
	$s = 1$	$s = 2$	$s = 4$	$s = 5$	$s = 6$	$s = 10$	$s = 11$	$s = 12$
Var0-R_7	+1	−1	−1	+1	+1	−1	+1	+1
Var1-R_5	−1	−1	−1	+1	+1	+1	+1	+1
Var2-R_4	−1	+1	−1	+1	+1	+1	−1	+1
Var3-R_3	−1	−1	+1	+1	+1	−1	−1	+1
Var4-R_3	−1	−1	+1	+1	+1	−1	−1	+1
Var5-R_3	−1	−1	+1	+1	+1	−1	−1	+1
Var6-R_3	−1	−1	+1	−1	+1	−1	−1	+1
Var7-R_1	−1	−1	−1	−1	+1	−1	+1	+1
Var8-R_6	−1	−1	−1	−1	+1	+1	+1	+1

Table 4.20 Ultimate HQ matrix for level_2

Reduct with variation	Attribute number ($Attr_s$)							
	$s = 1$	$s = 2$	$s = 4$	$s = 5$	$s = 6$	$s = 10$	$s = 11$	$s = 12$
Var0-Red_7	1.0	0.0	0.0	1.8	2.44	0.0	2.952	3.361
Var1-Red_5	0.0	0.0	0.0	1.0	1.8	2.44	2.952	3.361
Var2-Red_4	0.0	0.0	0.0	0.0	1.8	2.44	0.0	2.952
Var3-Red_3	0.0	0.0	1.0	1.8	2.44	0.0	0.0	2.952
Var4-Red_3	0.0	0.0	1.0	1.8	2.44	0.0	0.0	3.361
Var5-Red_3	0.0	0.0	1.0	1.8	2.95	0.0	0.0	2.952
Var6-Red_3	0.0	0.0	1.0	2.44	2.44	0.0	0.0	2.44
Var7-Red_1	0.0	0.0	0.0	0.0	1.8	0.0	1.8	1.8
Var8-Red_6	−1.0	−1.0	1.0	−1.0	1.0	1.0	1.0	1.0

reused in any other problem. The proposed method optimizes the range of values of linguistic labels used in each *reduct* and in each attribute at two different levels. It also focuses on building of an efficient classifier that is suitable for dynamic rule-base, with optimized value range of each attribute. It is also ascertained that classification accuracy due to the optimization of the linguistic labels either improves or maintains its original value, but never degrades.

Table 4.21 Optimal variation for attributes

Attribute	Variation
$Attr_0$	–
$Attr_1$	Var0
$Attr_2$	Var2
$Attr_3$	–
$Attr_4$	Var3/Var4/Var6/Var8
$Attr_5$	Var6
$Attr_6$	Var5
$Attr_7$	–
$Attr_8$	–
$Attr_9$	–
$Attr_{10}$	Var1
$Attr_{11}$	Var0
$Attr_{12}$	Var4

Table 4.22 Correlation of accuracy with no-variation and optimal variation

$Reduct$	Accuracy (no-variation) %	Accuracy (optimal variation) %
R_1	81.63	81.21
R_2	78.50	79.50
R_3	70.50	79.50
R_4	78.00	75.00
R_5	77.50	79.50
R_6	74.50	79.00
R_7	76.50	76.50
R_8	74.00	74.00

References

1. M. Barreno, B. Nelson, R. Sears, A.D. Joseph, J.D. Tygar, Can machine learning be secure?, in *Proceedings of the 2006 ACM Symposium on Information, Computer and Communications Security*, pp. 16–25 (2006)
2. I. Kononenko, Naive Bayesian classifier and continuous attributes. Informatica **16**(1), 1–8 (1992)
3. KDD Cup 1999 Data Data Set, UCI Machine Learning Repository. http://archive.ics.uci.edu/ml/datasets/KDD+Cup+1999+Data
4. S. Zanero, S.M. Savaresi, Unsupervised learning techniques for an intrusion detection system, in *SAC'04*, 14–17 Mar 2004
5. Y. Liao, Machine learning in intrusion detection. PhD Thesis, University of California (2005)
6. A. Patcha, J.-M. Park, An overview of anomaly detection techniques: existing solutions and latest technological trends. J. Comput. Netw. (2007)
7. T.P. Tran, P. Tsai, T. Jan, X. Kong, Network intrusion detection using machine learning and voting techniques, in *Machine Learning*, ed. by Y. Zhang. ISBN 978-953-307-033-9, Hard cover (InTech, 2010), 438 p

8. X. Xu, Adaptive intrusion detection based on machine learning: feature extraction, classifier construction and sequential pattern prediction. Int. J. Web Serv. Pract. **2**(1-2), 49–58 (2006)
9. X. Du, J. Zhai, K. Lv, *Algorithm Trading Using Q-Learning and Recurrent Reinforcement Learning*. Stanford University, Course CS 229 (Machine Learning), Final Projects (2009)
10. T. Kohri, K. Matsubayashi, M. Tokoro, An adaptive architecture for modular Q-learning, in *Proceedings of the Fifteenth International Joint Conference on Artificial Intelligence*, vol. 2. ISBN:1-555860-480-4 (Morgan Kaufmann Publishers Inc., San Francisco, pp. 820–825, 1997)
11. A.L. Servin, Distributed network defence and reinforcement learning. Thesis (2006)
12. Q. Zhu, T. Basar, Dynamic policy-based IDS configuration, in *Proceedings of the 48th IEEE Conference on Decision and Control, 2009 held jointly with the 2009 28th Chinese Control Conference. CDC/CCC 2009* (2009), pp. 8600–8605
13. A. Servin, D. Kudenko, Multi-agent reinforcement learning for intrusion detection, in *Proceedings of the 5th, 6th and 7th European Conference on Adaptive and Learning Agents and Multi-Agent Systems: Adaptation and Multi-Agent Learning* (Springer, Berlin, 2008), pp. 211–223
14. N. Sengupta, J. Sen, J. Sil, M. Saha, Designing of on line intrusion detection system using rough set theory and Q learning algorithm. Neurocomputing **111**, 161–168 (2013)
15. N. Sengupta, J. Sil, Comparison of different rule calculation method for rough set theory. Int. J. Inf. Electron. Eng. **2**(3) (2012)
16. J. Visumathi, K.L. Shunmuganathan, A computational intelligence for evaluation of intrusion detection system. Indian J. Sci. Technol. **4**(1), 0974–6846 (2011)
17. D.A. Karras, V. Zorkadis, Neural network techniques for improved intrusion detection in communication systems, in *Proceedings of the 5th WSES International Conference on Circuits, Systems, Communications and Computers* (CSCC 2001). ISBN: 960–8052-33-5 (2001)
18. S.G. Bhirud, V. Katkar, Novel architecture for intrusion-tolerant distributed intrusion detection system using packet filter firewall and state transition tables. Int. J. Comput. Appl. **8**(11) (2010)
19. D. Lee, D. Kim, J. Jung, Multi-stage intrusion detection system using hidden markov model algorithm. IEEE Int. Conf. Inf. Sci. Secur. 72–77 (2008)
20. D. Dal, S. Abraham, A. Abraham, S. Sanyal, M. Sanglikar, Evolution induced secondary immunity: an artificial immune system based intrusion detection system, in *IEEE, 7th Computer Information Systems & Industrial Management Applications*, pp. 65–70 (2008)
21. M.-Y. Su, K.-C. Chang, H.-F. Wei, C.-Y. Lin: A real-time network intrusion detection system based on incremental mining approach, in *IEEE International Conference on Intelligence and Security Informatics*, pp. 179–184 (2008)
22. M.H. Hansen, B. Yu, Model selection and the principle of minimum description length. J. Am. Stat. Assoc. **96**, 454 (2001)
23. L. Breiman, J. Friedman, R. Olshen, C. Stone, *Classification and Regression Trees* (CRC Press 1998)
24. J. Cannady, Applying CMAC-based on-line learning to intrusion detection, in *Proceedings of the IEEE-INNS-ENNS International Joint Conference on Neural Networks (IJCNN'00)*, vol. 5.ISBN:0–7695-0619-4 (IEEE Computer Society Washington, DC, USA, 2000)
25. W. Wang, X.-H. Guan, X.-L. Zhang, Modeling program behaviors by hidden Markov models for intrusion detection, in *Proceedings of the Third International Conference on Machine Learning and Cybernetics, Shanghai*, 26–29 Aug 2004
26. H. Tang, Z. Cao, Machine learning-based intrusion detection algorithms. J. Comput. Inf. Syst. **5**(6), 1825–1831 (2009)
27. D.L. Davies, D.W. Bouldin, A cluster separation measure. IEEE Trans. Patt. Recogn. Mach. Intell. **1**(2), 224–227 (1979)
28. M.A. Rassam, M.A. Maarof, A. Zainal, Intrusion detection system using unsupervised immune network clustering with reduced features. Int. J. Adv. Soft Comput. Appl. **2**(3) (2010)
29. M. Saha, J. Sil, N. Sengupta, Designing of an efficient classifier using hierarchical reinforcement learning, in *ICGST Conference on Computer Science and Engineering, Dubai, UAE*, 16–19 July 2012

30. A. Chouchoulas, Q. Shen, Rough set-aided keyword reduction for text categorisation. Appl Artif Intell **15**(9), 843–873 (2001)
31. N. Zhong, J. Dong, S. Ohsuga, Using rough sets with heuristics for feature selection. J. Intell. Inf. Syst. **16**, 199–214 (2001)
32. R. Jensen, Q. Shen, Fuzzy-rough sets for descriptive dimensionality reduction, in *Proceedings of the 11th International Conference on Fuzzy Systems* (2002), pp. 29–34
33. F. Abu-Amara, I. Abdel-Qader, Hybrid mammogram classification using rough set and fuzzy classifier. Int. J. Biomed. Imaging **2009** (2009)
34. Nsl-kdd data set for network-based intrusion detection systems. http://nsl.cs.unb.ca/KDD/NSL-KDD.html, Mar 2009
35. M. Baykal-Gürsoy, Semi-markov decision processes. Probab. Eng. Inf. Sci. **21**, 635–657 (2007)
36. H. Xiong, S. Shekhar, P.-N. Tan, V. Kumar, Exploiting a support-based upper bound of Pearson's correlation coefficient for efficiently identifying strongly correlated pairs, in KDD'04, 22–25 Aug 2004
37. S.M. Kakade, On the sample complexity of reinforcement learning. Ph.D. thesis (Gatsby Computational Neuroscience Unit, University College London, 2003)
38. B.R. Leffler, M.L. Littman, T. Edmunds, Efficient reinforcement learning with re locatable action models, in *Proceedings of the Twenty-Second Conference on Artificial Intelligence* (2007), p 572577

Chapter 5
Conclusions and Future Research

Data mining is an integrated process to deal with cleaning, integration, selection, transformation, extraction of data, evaluation of pattern and knowledge acquisition management. The exponential growth of data opens up new challenges to extracting knowledge from large repositories consisting of vague, incomplete and hidden information. Data mining research attracted people working in diverse disciplines. However, the existing methods lack a comprehensive and systematic approach to tackle several problems in data mining techniques, many of which are interrelated. The book attempts to develop data mining algorithms to address the problems in an integrated way, considering issues with discretization, dimension reduction and machine learning domains. The proposed algorithms are applied to design an autonomous intrusion detection system (IDS) to classify on-line network traffic data. Performance of the system is dependent equally on the result of each of the processes and so evaluated at the end of each stage of data processing, demonstrating their mutual dependence.

5.1 Essence of the Proposed Methods

Rough set theory (RST), pioneered by Pawlak [1, 2], has been used in this monograph as a data mining tool in developing different algorithms. RST has the ability to handle vague large data set, even when no other sources of the data are available. RST is computationally simpler and inexpensive. Fuzzy set theory, pioneered by Zadeh [3], is another method to handle vague data set. Here, fuzzy set theory has been merged with RST to overcome the limitations of both of the approaches [4]. Fuzzy-Rough set (FZ-RS) theory is applied on continuous data set whereas RST is only applicable for discrete data set. Therefore, continuous and discrete domain data set are analyzed separately by applying FZ-RS theory and RST respectively for discovering knowledge from NSL KDD network data set to build the IDS.

Genetic algorithm (GA), invented by Holland [5], has been used in the monograph as an optimization algorithm to search optimum set of features sufficient to classify a given decision table. GA always finds the global optimum solution and so improves

© Springer Nature Singapore Pte Ltd. 2020
N. Sengupta and J. Sil, *Intrusion Detection*, Cognitive Intelligence and Robotics,
https://doi.org/10.1007/978-981-15-2716-6_5

classification accuracy and reduces system complexity. Particle swarm optimization (PSO), which is another optimization algorithm developed by Kennedy et al. [6–9], iteratively attempts to improve the candidate solution. PSO has fast convergence speed but often get trapped at local minima. PSO is used here as a tool of optimization in the development of a real-time IDS, containing vague and time-varying data.

Cut generation [10] is one kind of thresholding method [11] applied for partitioning continuous data depending on some constraints [11]. In the monograph, cut is applied to discretize continuous attribute values based on the class labels of the data set. Cut is used to learn the behavior of the system and classifying on-line network data accurately for its computational efficiency.

RST is integrated with simulated annealing method developed by Kirkpatric et al. [12]. Simulated Annealing rests on the principle of thermodynamic equilibrium of metal. It is a heuristic based random search algorithm that finds global optimum solution. This has been used in the monograph to optimize the number of clusters with respect to each attribute. It is important to note that in classical FCM algorithm [13, 14], number of clusters needs to be provided.

Q-learning as a reinforcement learning [15] method is applied for dynamic learning of data. Modified Q-learning algorithm is proposed while developing the adaptive IDS using the structure of Q-learning. Speed of Modified-Q-Learning algorithm is enhanced with the development of Hierarchical-Q-Learning method, where the complete problem is divided into sub-problems and each of them contributes to achieve the best solution.

5.2 Outstanding Issues

In Chapter 1 background of the work with its aims and objectives are presented. In this chapter, review of the existing works relevant to the monograph are discussed. Issues and challenges of Intrusion Detection System, different methods of discretization, shortcomings of discretization, attribute and instance reduction techniques, and reinforcement learning have been presented here. Methods of feature selection, which effectively reduces dimensionality of data has been presented by giving emphasis on RST and Fuzzy Rough set theory based approaches. In intrusion detection domain, application of machine learning approaches are not new and a wide research area already has developed by researchers using different learning paradigm. Reinforcement Learning, dynamic learning and more specifically Q-learning based methods are studied for its application in building dynamic IDS. Other dynamic learning proposals are presented briefly, though a few left for their limited scope of application in this monograph.

In Chapter 2, efficient way of discretization applied on intrusion detection domain has been proposed. There are different discretization methods and not a single method of discretization has been considered as a unique method for any type of database. Rather, it has been found that a particular method of discretization is suitable for a specific database. Center spread encoding technique is employed on network traffic data set for discretization of conditional attribute values based on class labels. Classification accuracy using different classifiers are compared before applying and after applying the proposed discretization method. Evaluation of different metrics like correctly classified instances and different statistical measure establishes the fact that the proposed discretization method produces minimum information loss. It has been proved that adequate number of cut points has been developed and used for discretization of all continuous attributes which maintains consistency [16] of the decision system after discretization. After discretization process is over, it has been observed that integrity of each object is maintained. Therefore, it can be concluded that unlike other existing method of discretization, cut based center spread encoding technique for discretization method does not generate information loss and consistency in the data set and classification accuracy has also been achieved with satisfactory results.

Other two discretization methods based on machine learning approaches have been proposed in Chapter 2. Optimized Equal Width Interval (OEWI) and Split and Merge Interval (SMI) are applied for discretization of data and preserve consistency in the data set. The claim is established by proving a theorem and so equally applicable for other data sets and satisfactory results have been achieved. Accuracy of classifiers in almost all cases is achieved 98%, comparable with other discretization methods.

In Chapter 3, data reduction has been focused which is an important task for efficient data analysis. Motivation of data reduction lies in a reduced representation of a large volume of data without sacrificing the integrity of data. Feature reduction technique is so important that computation complexity gets reduced with reduction of attribute but information of the system is retained. In this chapter, dimension reduction has been performed separately for discrete domain and continuous domain data set. In discrete domain, RST has been established with satisfactory outcome. In continuous domain, the limitation of the existing Rough Set based attribute reduction is explained with a view to design a new algorithm DIM-RED-GA by hybridization of Fuzzy and Rough Set techniques. Information loss due to implementation of Rough Set approximation has been overcome by applying combined Fuzzy-Rough technique. Genetic Algorithm (GA) is a well-known tool for intelligent search and optimization which is used in DIM—RED—GA technique to find the optimum *reduct* for classification. The problem of having stuck in the local optima of Fuzzy-Rough QuickReduct (FRQR) [17] technique has been overcome by implementing GA. It has been noticed that by implementing DIM—RED—GA technique, achieved length of *reduct* is less or equal compared to other classical methods and classification accuracy acquired is also recommendable.

For instance reduction, SAFC algorithm [18, 19] has been modified first for removing randomness in data clustering with respect to each conditional attribute. Assuming different initial number of clusters, DB indices are calculated showing better performance of the modified SAFC algorithm compared to the SAFC algorithm. Modified SAFC algorithm is extended using RST to eliminate redundant and less informative instances. Reduced set of instances provides classification accuracy good enough compared to the original data set. Application of instance reduction method has importance, where data set is really high as far as computation time and complexity are concerned.

Machine Learning is an integrated area of data mining where researchers contributed to develop new learning algorithms for building real time systems. In intrusion domain, supervised learning and unsupervised learning attracted many researchers but there are more scopes of further research on reinforcement learning. In extended Q-Learning algorithm discretization, *reduct* generation and classification issues are integrated using RST and applied to develop on-line IDS which can classify the network traffic with as high as 98% classification accuracy. The proposed technique of dimension reduction helps in identifying the most appropriate features to sustain high classification accuracy at low computation overhead [20–22]. In the monograph, different cuts are learnt by the proposed Extended Q-Learning algorithm for discretization of conditional attributes, based on which features are selected resulting in highest classification accuracy. It is interesting to note that classification accuracy has wide variation for the selection of two successive cuts. However, choice of different cuts for different attributes offers the best result in classification. Effectiveness of the system in the detection of real time network intrusion is examined with data sets of using correlation.

In the book, concept of Hierarchical-Q-Learning has been highlighted and a modified Hierarchical-Q-Learning algorithm is proposed. The proposed method optimizes the range of values of linguistic labels of the rule set in two levels. In the first level, linguistic labels of *reducts* and in the second level the same for attributes are achieved. The objective of the proposed method is to build an efficient classifier that is suitable for dynamic rule-base, with optimized value range of each rule. In addition, discretization of data set is avoided in this approach, since actions are mapped as range of linguistic variables as applied on continuous domain. It is also ascertained that accuracy of classification after optimizing the linguistic labels either improves or is at par in absence of optimization.

NSL KDD data set is explained in Annexure. Finally as a remark it is worth to mention that though the book mainly concentrates on intrusion domain data set, others standard data sets are also equally applicable and verified using the proposed algorithms.

5.3   Future Research Directions

Detection of an unmatched class is an important issue in classical pattern recognition technique. In the detection of network intrusion, it is often found that the existing data set does not match with any of the existing class labels. This requires adding a new class label for the current data. In the future research adding new class labels may be treated as learning of new information which might have a new direction to the traditional pattern recognition theory. In traditional research, it is often presumed that the dynamic range of the data maintain a uniform moving average. Thus, when a data stream goes outside the dynamic range, it is treated as noisy. However, there exists possibilities of having high data variability as network intrusion, sometimes is vulnerable and this may not be predicted so easily as it is handled usually. Classifying network traffic with high data variability thus needs special attention for future research. One approach might be to employ an ensemble classification realized by different techniques, the classification outcome of which may be fused to improve accuracy, particularly when the data variation goes beyond expected values. Minimum change of rule set depending on the data set may be one of the solutions.

Data preprocessing like missing value prediction, handling of heterogeneous transformation of data to reduce computational overhead are the new challenges where researchers can contribute.

Intrusion detection, in general, does not include prevention of intrusions. So prevention methods using data mining techniques would be a challenging topic to protect network without disturbing the activities of the systems. Different types of attacks (specifically DoS attacks) can be diagnosed considering behavior of anomalous protocol, so network protocol analysis is important to identify the attack at very low level of the network. For intrusion detection, Target detection has demonstrated as one of the most strong, valid methods.

References

1. Z. Pawlak, *Rough Sets: Theoretical Aspects of Reasoning About Data*, (Kluwer Academic Publishers, Boston, London, Dordrecht 229, 1991)
2. Z. Pawlak, Rough set theory and its applications to data analysis. Cybern. Syst. **29**, 661–688 (1998)
3. L.A. Zadeh, Fuzzy sets. Inf. Control **8**, 338–353 (1965)
4. Y. Rama Devi, P. Venu Gopal, P.S.V.S. Sai Prasad, Fuzzy rough data reduction using SVD. Int. J. Comput. Electr. Eng. **3**(3) June (2011)
5. J. H. Holland, *Adaptation in Natural and Artificial Systems*, 2nd edn. (MIT Press, Cambridge, MA), (1992) 1st edn. (University of Michigan Press) (1975/1992)
6. J. Kennedy, The behavior of particles. The Seventh Annual Conference on Evolutionary Programming, (March 1998), p. 581–591
7. J. Kennedy, The particle swarm: Social adaptation of knowledge. Proceedings of the 1997 IEEE international conference on evolutionary computation, Indianapolis, Indiana, IEEE Service Center, Piscataway, NJ, 303–308 1997
8. J. Kennedy, R.C. Eberhart, A discrete binary version of the particle swarm algorithm. Proceedings of the 1997 Conference on Systems, Man, and Cybernetics, IEEE Service Center, Piscataway, NJ, 4104–4109 1997
9. J. Kennedy, R.C. Eberhart, Particle swarm optimization. Proceedings of the 1995 IEEE international conference on neural networks, IEEE Service Center, Piscataway, NJ, Perth, Australia, 1942–1948 1995
10. H. Liu, F. Hussain, C.L. Tan, M. Dash, Discretization: An enabling technique. Data Min. Knowl. Discov. **6**, 393–423 (2002)
11. Y. Ge, F. Cao, R.F. Duan, Impact of discretization methods on the rough set-based classification of remotely sensed images. Int. J. Digit. Earth **4**(4), 330–346 (2011)
12. S.C.G. Kirkpatrick, C.D. Gelatt, M. Vecchi, Optimization by simulated annealing. Science **220**(1983), 49–58 (1983)
13. N.R. Pal, J.C. Bezdek, On cluster validity for the fuzzy c-means model. IEEE Trans. Fuzzy Syst. **3**, 370–379 (1995)

14. Doulaye Dembele, P. Kaster, Fuzzy c-means method for clustering microarray data. Bioinformatics **19**(8), 973–980 (2003)
15. C.J.C.H. Watkins, P. Dayan, Q-learning, machine learning, **8**(3–4), 279–292 (1992)
16. S. Mazumder, T. Sharma, R. Mitra, N. Sengupta, J. Sil. *Chapter 62 Generation of Sufficient Cut Points to Discretize Network Traffic Data Sets*, (Springer Science and Business Media LLC, 2012)
17. J. R. Anaraki, M. Eftekhari, Improving fuzzy-rough quick reduct for feature selection. IEEE 19th Iranian conference on electrical engineering (ICEE), 1–6 (2011)
18. X.Y. Wang, G. Whitwell, J.M. Garibaldi, The application of a simulated annealing fuzzy clustering algorithm for cancer diagnosis. In the proceedings of IEEE 4th international conference on intelligent systems design and application, Budapest, Hungary, Aug 26–28 (2004), pp. 467–472
19. S. Bandyopadhyay, Simulated annealing for fuzzy clustering: variable representation, evolution of the number of clusters and remote sensing application. Machine Intelligence Unit, Indian Statistical Institute (unpublished personal communication) 2003
20. S. M. Kakade, On the sample complexity of reinforcement learning. PhD thesis, Gatsby Computational Neuroscience Unit, University College London, 2003
21. B. R. Leffler, M. L. Littman, T. Edmunds, Efficient reinforcement learning with re locatable action models. Proceedings of the twenty-second conference on artificial intelligence (2007), pp. p. 572–577
22. L. Panait, S. Luke, Cooperative multi-agent learning: The state of the art. Auton. Agents Multi-Agent Syst. **11**(3), 387–434 (2005). Springer

Annexure

Network Traffic Data Set

KDD'99 data set has been used by the researchers for a long time for intrusion detection domain. As it has some inherent problems mentioned in [1], NSL-KDD data set is being used by the present-day researchers for this domain. This new version of the KDD data set has some problems discussed by McHugh [2] and it deviates from existing real networks. This data set can be used as an effective benchmark data set by researchers to compare different intrusion detection methods because of the lack of public data sets for network-based IDSs. NSL-KDD data set has been considered in the book because it has the following advantages over the original KDD data set:

- Proposed test sets are free from duplicate records.
- Redundant records are not there in the training data set.
- As original KDD'99 data size is too big, researchers need to select the records for establishing their theory from the whole data set. In case of NSL-KDD, whole data set can be used for evaluation of classification accuracy for different machine learning techniques, which makes it more efficient.
- Size of the train and test sets is reasonable to run the experiments on the complete set without the need to randomly select a small portion. As a result of it, evaluation results of different research works will be consistent and comparable.

In NSL-KDD dataset, each object has 42 attributes; out of 42 attributes, 41 are conditional attributes and 1 is decision attribute which has two class levels, "anomaly" and "normal". Out of 41 attributes, 34 are continuous and 7 are discrete attributes.

Detail statistics of the continuous attributes for 11,850 objects have been mentioned in Table A.1. Statistical properties of these attributes have been derived using Tanagra software.

Detailed statistics of seven conditional discrete attributes and one decisional discrete attributes for 11,850 objects have been mentioned in Table A.2a–h. Statistical properties of these attributes have been derived using Tanagra software.

© Springer Nature Singapore Pte Ltd. 2020

N. Sengupta and J. Sil, *Intrusion Detection*, Cognitive Intelligence and Robotics,
https://doi.org/10.1007/978-981-15-2716-6

Table A.1 Statistical value of each continuous attribute

Attribute	Min	Max	Average	Std-dev	Std-dev/avg
Duration	0	57,715	415.4398	1919.4416	4.6203
src_bytes	0	6.28256E7	19,456.4413	651,986.5187	33.5101
dst_bytes	0	1.28865E6	1228.1052	23,896.0319	19.4576
wrong_fragment	0	3	0.0160	0.1964	12.2479
Urgent	0	3	0.0014	0.0503	37.2530
Hot	0	101	0.1902	1.2224	6.4265
num_failed_logins	0	4	0.0412	0.2054	4.9877
num_compromised	0	796	0.2277	10.0258	44.0346
root_shell	0	1	0.0043	0.0655	15.2109
su_attempted	0	2	0.0005	0.0290	57.3668
num_root	0	878	0.2181	11.0909	50.8621
num_file_creations	0	100	0.0162	0.9332	57.5961
num_shells	0	5	0.0022	0.0662	30.1764
num_access_files	0	4	0.0039	0.0768	19.7749
num_outbound_cmds	0	0	0.0000	0.0000	99999.0000
count	0	511	94.1161	153.4190	1.6301
srv_count	0	511	48.2695	119.2139	2.4698
serror_rate	0	1	0.1138	0.3059	2.6875
srv_serror_rate	0	1	0.1146	0.3092	2.6985
serror_rate	0	1	0.2743	0.4304	1.5688
srv_rerror_rate	0	1	0.2684	0.4302	1.6033
sarne_srv_rate	0	1	0.7530	0.3990	0.5299
diff_srv_rate	0	1	0.1571	0.3388	2.1557
srv_diff_host_rate	0	1	0.0968	0.2787	2.8799
dst_host_count	1	255	213.9454	82.2037	0.3842
dst_host_srv_cou nt	1	255	117.5416	106.5634	0.9066
dst_host_same_srv_rate	0	1	0.5396	0.4234	0.7846
dst_host_diff_srv_rate	0	1	0.1490	0.2888	1.9382
dst_host_same_src_port_rate	0	1	0.2065	0.3792	1.8363
dst host srv diff_hont rate	0	1	0.0245	0.1142	4.6693
dst_host_serror_rate	0	1	0.1042	0.2651	2.5445
dst_host_srv_serror_rate	0	1	0.1067	0.2785	2.6107
dst_host_rerror_rate	0	1	0.2640	0.3773	1.4296
dst_host_srv_rerror_rate	0	1	0.2522	0.403	1.5980

Table A.2 **a** Statistical value of "Protocol-type" attribute, **b** statistical value of "service" attribute, **c** statistical value of "flag" attribute, **d** statistical value of "land" attribute, **e** statistical value of "logged_in" attribute, **f** statistical value of "is_host_login" attribute, **g** statistical value of "is_guest_login" attribute, **h** statistical value of "class" attribute

(a)

Attribute	Gini	Distribution			
		Values	Count	Percent	Histogram
protocol_type	0.4269	tcp	8632	72.84 %	
		udp	2238	18.89 %	
		icmp	980	8.27 %	

(b)

Values	Count	Percent	Histogram
telnet	1617	13.65 %	
private	1927	16.26 %	
http	1400	11.81 %	
imap4	304	2.57 %	
ftp_data	718	6.06 %	
other	817	6.89 %	
ctf	38	0.32 %	
pop_3	1007	8.50 %	
ftp	672	5.67 %	
domain_u	550	4.64 %	
domain	45	0.38 %	
eco_i	261	2.20 %	
ecr_i	701	5.92 %	
finger	93	0.78 %	
name	34	0.29 %	
smtp	424	3.58 %	
vmnet	38	0.32 %	
mtp	27	0.23 %	
bgp	45	0.38 %	
exec	25	0.21 %	
sunrpc	152	1.28 %	
uucp_path	39	0.33 %	
iso_tsap	46	0.39 %	
echo	35	0.30 %	
auth	50	0.42 %	
hostnames	21	0.18 %	

(continued)

Table A.2 (continued)

					Histogram
		courier	37	0.31 %	·
		uucp	50	0.42 %	·
service	0.9135	daytime	25	0.21 %	·
		nntp	13	0.11 %	·
		netstat	17	0.14 %	·
		urp_i	12	0.10 %	·
		http_443	33	0.28 %	·
		csnet_ns	32	0.27 %	·
		login	25	0.21 %	·
		klogin	16	0.14 %	·
		whois	39	0.33 %	·
		time	30	0.25 %	·
		link	35	0.30 %	·
		discard	24	0.20 %	·
		gopher	32	0.27 %	·
		supdup	23	0.19 %	·
		netbios_ns	25	0.21 %	·
		systat	30	0.25 %	·
		netbios_dgm	22	0.19 %	·
		kshell	17	0.14 %	·
		efs	28	0.24 %	·
		nnsp	39	0.33 %	·
		ssh	19	0.16 %	·
		netbios_ssn	12	0.10 %	·
		Z39_50	45	0.38 %	·
		IRC	13	0.11 %	·
		ntp_u	1	0.01 %	·
		X11	15	0.13 %	·
		pm_dump	16	0.14 %	·
		ldap	15	0.13 %	·
		remote_job	3	0.03 %	·
		sql_net	12	0.10 %	·
		shell	1	0.01 %	·
		tim_i	6	0.05 %	·
		pop_2	1	0.01 %	·
		tftp_u	1	0.01 %	·

(c)

Values	Count	Percent	Histogram
SF	7278	61.42 %	
S3	249	2.10 %	
SH	73	0.62 %	·
REJ	1852	15.63 %	

(continued)

Table A.2 (continued)

flag	0.5840	S0	1033	8.72 %	
		RSTO	658	5.55 %	
		RSTR	668	5.64 %	
		RSTOS0	2	0.02 %	
		S1	18	0.15 %	
		S2	15	0.13 %	
		OTH	4	0.03 %	

(d)

		Values	Count	Percent	Histogram
land	0.0012	0	11843	99.94 %	
		1	7	0.06 %	

(e)

		Values	Count	Percent	Histogram
logged_in	0.3781	1	2999	25.31 %	
		0	8851	74.69 %	

(f)

		Values	Count	Percent	Histogram
is_host_login	0.0019	0	11839	99.91 %	
		1	11	0.09 %	

(g)

		Values	Count	Percent	Histogram
is_guest_login	0.1002	0	11223	94.71 %	
		1	627	5.29 %	

(h)

		Values	Count	Percent	Histogram
class	0.2972	anomaly	9698	81.84 %	
		normal	2152	18.16 %	

Graphical representation of the values of each attribute is shown in Figure A.1 using WEKA software.

Description of each attribute is given in Table A.3.

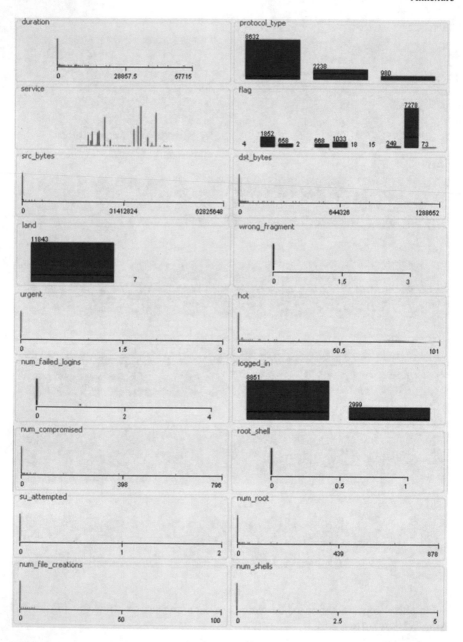

Figure A.1 Graphical representation of values of each attribute

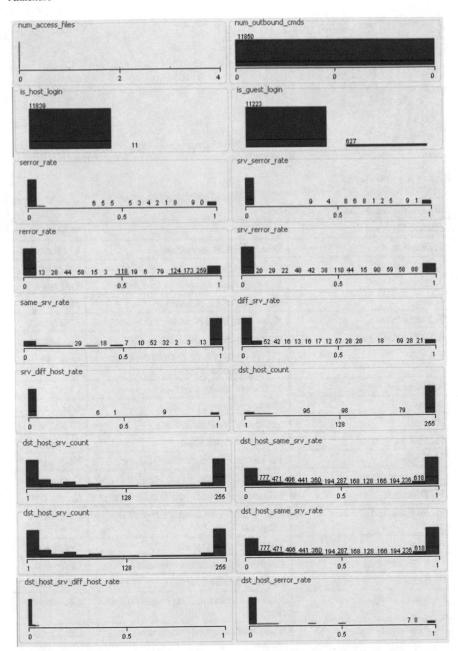

Figure A.1 (continued)

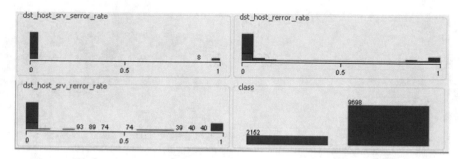

Figure A.1 (continued)

Table A.3 Description of each attribute

Feature	Description	Type
1. Duration	Duration of the connection	Continuous
2. Protocol type	Connection protocol (e.g., tcp, udp)	Discrete
3. Service	Destination service (e.g., telnet, ftp)	Discrete
4. Flag	Status flag of the connection	Discrete
5. Source bytes	Bytes sent from source to destination	Continuous
6. Destination bytes	Bytes sent from destination to source	Continuous
7. Land	1 if the connection is from/to the same host/port; 0 otherwise	Discrete
8. Wrong fragment	Number of wrong fragments	Continuous
9. Urgent	Number of urgent packets	Continuous
10. Hot	Number of "hot" indicators	Continuous
11. Failed logins	Number of failed logins	Continuous
12. Logged in	1 if successfully logged in; 0 otherwise	Discrete
13. # compromised	Number of "compromised" conditions	Continuous
14. Root shell	1 if root shell is obtained; 0 otherwise	Continuous
15. Su attempted	1 if "su root" command attempted; 0 otherwise	Continuous
16. # root	Number of root accesses	Continuous
17. # file creations	Number of file creation operations	Continuous
18. # shells	Number of shell prompts	Continuous
19. # access files	Number of operations on access control files	Continuous
20. # outbound cmds	Number of outbound commands in an ftp session	Continuous

(continued)

Table A.3 (continued)

Feature	Description	Type
21. Is host login	1 if the login belongs to the "host" list; 0 otherwise	Discrete
22. Is guest login	1 if the login is a "guest" login; 0 otherwise	Discrete
23. Count	Number of connections to the same host as the current connection in the past two seconds	Continuous
24. Srv count	Number of connections to the same service as the current connection in the past two seconds	Continuous
25. Serror rate	% of connections that have "SYN" errors	Continuous
26. Srv serror rate	% of connections that have "SYN" errors in Srv count feature	Continuous
27. Rerror rate	% of connections that have "REJ" errors	Continuous
28. Srv rerror rate	% of connections that have "REJ" errors in Srv count feature	Continuous
29. Same srv rate	% of connections to the same service	Continuous
30. Diff srv rate	% of connections to different services	Continuous
31. Srv diff host rate	% of connections to different hosts	Continuous
32. Dst host count	Count of connections having the same destination host	Continuous
33. Dst host srv count	Count of connections having the same destination host and using the same service	Continuous
34. Dst host same srv rate	% of connections having the same destination host and using the same service	Continuous
35. Dst host diff srv rate	% of different services on the current host	Continuous
36. Dst host same src port rate	% of connections to the current host having the same src port	Continuous
37. Dst host srv diff host rate	% of connections to the same service coming from different hosts	Continuous
38. Dst host serror rate	% of connections to the current host that have an S0 error	Continuous
39. Dst host srv serror rate	% of connections to the current host and specified service that have an S0 error	Continuous
40. Dst host rerror rate	% of connections to the current host that have an RST error	Continuous
41. Dst host srv rerror rate	% of connections to the current host and specified service that have an RST error	Continuous

References

1. M. Tavallaee, E. Bagheri, W. Lu, A. Ghorbani, A detailed analysis of the KDD CUP 99 data set, Submitted to *Second IEEE Symposium on Computational Intelligence for Security and Defense Applications (CISDA)* (2009)
2. J. McHugh, Testing intrusion detection systems: a critique of the 1998 and 1999 Darpa intrusion detection system evaluations as performed by Lincoln laboratory. ACM Trans. Inf. Syst. Secur. **3**(4), 262–294 (2000)

© Springer Nature Singapore Pte Ltd. 2020
N. Sengupta and J. Sil, *Intrusion Detection*, Cognitive Intelligence and Robotics,
https://doi.org/10.1007/978-981-15-2716-6

Subject Index

A

Absorption, 2, 17
Absorption and extension law, 17
Absorption law, 2, 17, 54
Actual value, 32, 75
Analytic engine, 3
AND, 54, 55
Anomaly, 1, 5, 15, 16, 18, 28–30, 37, 39, 74, 76, 83, 119
Anomaly detection, 4, 5
Antivirus, 1
Apriori, 4, 10
Attribute dependency, 10, 13, 17, 50, 55, 68, 71, 79
Attribute reduction, 8, 47, 79, 115
Availability, 1, 3
Availability of data, 1

B

Bagging, 77
Bayesian formalism, 6
BayesNet, 77
Binary cuts, 13
Bin medians method, 7
Binning process, 12
Bottom-up merging process, 12
Bottom-up methods, 12
Boundaries, 7, 10, 11, 15, 29, 50, 60
Boundary region, 50
Boundary value, 7
Build an IDS, 3

C

Centralizing, 4
Centre, 16, 32, 33, 68, 70
Centre-spread encoding method, 32
Centre-spread encoding technique, 32, 33
Child nodes, 55, 56, 58
ChiMerge, 12
ChiMerge procedure, 12
Chi-square, 12
Chi-square test, 12
Chromosome, 63, 64
Class-Attribute Dependent Discretizer (CADD), 13
Classification, 2, 8, 11, 15, 17, 39, 47, 72, 76, 79, 85, 88, 89, 95, 97, 99, 101, 106, 115–117
Classification accuracy, 2, 16–18, 27, 40, 41, 47, 48, 67, 68, 76–79, 85, 86, 88, 89, 92, 94–101, 106, 108, 114–116, 119
Classifier, 2, 14–18, 28, 39, 47, 72, 73, 75–77, 79, 95–98, 108, 115, 116
Classify, 1, 2, 15, 17, 83, 96, 113, 116
Clustering, 10, 11, 60, 67, 68, 79
Clustering algorithms, 9–11
C-means, 11, 60, 67, 114
Comparison of accuracy, 74
Complexity, 1, 2, 6, 16–18, 67, 79, 95, 114–116
Computational efficiency, 8, 114
Computer emergency response team, 1
Computer virus, 1
Computing environment, 8
Concept hierarchies, 8, 106, 116
Conditional attributes, 10, 16–18, 27–30, 34, 48, 50–52, 55–57, 61, 86, 88, 90, 92, 97, 104, 115, 116, 119
Confidentiality, 3
Confusion matrix, 17, 47, 75, 76
Consistency, 17, 18, 27, 37, 38, 40, 115

© Springer Nature Singapore Pte Ltd. 2020
N. Sengupta and J. Sil, *Intrusion Detection*, Cognitive Intelligence and Robotics,
https://doi.org/10.1007/978-981-15-2716-6

Continuous attributes, 2, 11–13, 28–30, 32,
    34, 38, 39, 75, 79, 88, 93, 95, 98, 99,
    101, 106, 114, 115, 119, 120
Convergence, 114
Correctly classified instances, 40, 73, 115
Correct predictions, 8
Correlation, 3, 28, 101, 104, 109, 116
Crisp equivalence class, 59
Crossing over point, 63
Crossover Procedure, 63
Cross validation model, 73
Cross validation technique, 39
Cryptographic techniques, 3
Cryptography, 1
Cut generation, 17, 30, 34, 39, 85, 106, 114
Cut generation method, 28, 85
Cut point, 11, 13, 17, 28–32, 34, 86, 115
Cyber-attacks, 1

D
Data analysis, 6, 8, 27, 50, 115
Data cleaning, 6
Data clustering, 10, 115
Data collection, 3
Data cubes, 8
Data extraction, v
Data integration, 8
Data mining, 1, 7, 8, 16, 27, 59, 113, 116,
    117
Data preprocessing, 3, 6, 27, 117
Data reduction, 8, 47, 115
Data transformation, 6, 7
Data warehousing, 8
Davies-Bouldin (DB), 77, 79, 115
Davies-Bouldin Validity Index, 77
DB index, 78, 79
Decision attribute, 16, 28–30, 34, 50–52, 56,
    57, 60, 61, 70, 119
Decision class, 28, 94
Decision table, 29, 77
Decision tree, 6, 13
Decision tree building process, 11
Decision tree induction method, 6
Decryption, 1
Degrees of membership, 10
Delete_centre, 70
Denial of service, 5
Denoising, 6
Digital signatures, 3
Dimensionality reduction, 9, 17, 18, 52, 58,
    71, 76
Dimensionality reduction algorithm, 66

Dimensionality reduction techniques, 9
Dimension reduction, 8, 9, 17, 18, 47, 48, 72,
    76, 79, 113, 115, 116
DIM-RED-GA, 76, 79, 115
Discernibility function, 2, 52, 54
Discernibility matrix, 10, 17, 51–53, 72, 88
Discernible pair, 30–32
Discover knowledge, 1
Discrete, 2, 7, 16, 18, 27, 29, 32, 34, 89, 98,
    119, 126, 127
Discrete data, 2, 16, 27, 59, 113
Discrete domain, 72, 79, 113, 115
Discrete intervals, 12
Discrete value mapping, 32
Discretization, 2, 11–13, 16–18, 27–29, 32,
    34, 36–40, 47, 79, 86, 88, 90, 93, 95,
    98, 99, 101, 106, 113–116
Discretization algorithms, 12, 38
Discriminating, 2, 8, 38
Distributed denial of service, 5
Distributed Intrusion Detection System
    (DIDS), 3
DoS attacks, 117
Dynamic, 1, 5, 11, 13–15, 18, 34, 35, 60, 85,
    114, 116
Dynamic classification, 15
Dynamic data, 15
Dynamic learning, 14, 114
Dynamic learning classifier, 15
Dynamic methods, 5, 11
Dynamic rule-base, 108, 116

E
Eavesdropping, 5
Encryption, 1
Entropy, 11, 13
Entropy-based method, 11, 13
Entropy heuristic, 13
Entropy/MDL, 13
Entropy value, 13
Environment, 14, 15, 98, 106
Equal-frequency, 12
Equal-width, 12
Equivalence class, 49, 50, 59
Error-based, 11
Error rate, 76
Evaluative feedback, 14
Exhaustive, 1, 2
Expansion law, 2, 55
Exploitation, 14, 15
Exploration, 14, 15
Exponential growth, 8, 113

F
False negative, 75
False positive, 42, 75
False positive rate, 42
Feature selection, 2, 9, 10, 114
Filter approach, 9
Final DB Index, 78
Final Q matrix, 87, 88, 94, 95, 98, 101, 103, 105
Final reward matrix, 87–89, 92, 94, 97, 98, 101–103, 105, 106, 108
Firewall, 1
Fitness function, 37, 60
Flat files, 8
F-measure, 42, 74
Frequency count, 2
Fuzzy, 17, 18, 47, 59, 60, 95–98, 113–115
Fuzzy-C, 60
Fuzzy cluster, 59
Fuzzy clustering, 10, 11, 68
Fuzzy-C-Means (FCM), 11, 60, 67, 114
Fuzzy C-means clustering algorithm, 11, 60, 67
Fuzzy equivalence class, 59
Fuzzy Inference System (FIS), 60, 61
Fuzzy membership, 70
Fuzzy-Rough, 17, 47, 58, 59, 79, 115
Fuzzy-Rough dependency, 60, 63
Fuzzy-Rough-GA, 60, 61, 63
Fuzzy-Rough positive region, 59
Fuzzy-Rough-Quick-Reduct, 17, 79, 115
Fuzzy Rough Set based Quick Reduct (FRQR), 47, 76, 79, 115
Fuzzy-Rough Set (FZ-RS), 18, 58–60, 63, 79, 96, 113
Fuzzy sets, 58, 59

G
Generalization, 8
Genetic Algorithms (GA), 3, 11, 17, 18, 47, 58, 60, 63, 64, 77, 79, 96, 113, 115
Genetic programming, 3
Geodesic distances, 9
Global best position, 35
Global discretization method, 11
Global methods, 11
Global optimization, 68
Goals and errors, 13
Goodness of i-th interval, 13
Greedy optimization processes, 9
Greedy search algorithm, 9
Group confidence, 35

H
Hacking, 1
Hard clustering, 10
Hashing algorithms, 27
Hashing function, 16
Heterogeneity, 8
Heterogeneous, 3, 117
Heuristic, 17, 30, 40, 114
Heuristic based approach, 17
Heuristic rule, 29
Hierarchical, 10, 18, 95–98, 104–106, 114, 116
Hierarchical level, 95, 106
Hierarchical method, 96
Hierarchical Q-learning, 18, 83, 95–97
Hierarchical Reinforcement Learning (HRL), 18, 83, 95, 106
Hierarchical reward matrix, 97
Higher dimensionality, 9
Holland, 113
Homogeneity, 8, 16, 28
Host-based, 3
HQ matrix, 98, 105
Hybridization, 10, 115
Hypothesis, 3
Hypothyroidism, 76, 77
Hypothyroidism dataset, 16

I
Incident-analysts, 4
Incomplete, 10, 113
Inconsistency, 6, 7, 16, 17, 27, 34, 37, 40
Inconsistency handling, 2
Inconsistent, 2, 7, 27, 34, 37
Incorrectly classified instances, 40, 73
Indiscernibility relation, 49, 52, 57
Indiscernible, 10, 49, 56
Indispensable attribute, 2, 17, 52, 72, 76
Inertial weight, 35
Inference-based tools, 6
Information gain, 13
Information loss, 16, 18, 40, 47, 76, 115
Initial DB index, 78
Initial HQ matrix, 98
Initial Q-matrix, 87, 92, 97
Initial Reward matrix, 86–89, 94, 97–99, 105, 107
Instance based k nearest neighbor (IBK), 77
Instance reduction, 17, 47, 67, 77, 79, 114, 115
Integrity, 1, 3, 40, 51, 52, 115
Interception, 5
Internet of Things, 1

Interpret data, 6
Intrusion, 3–5, 15, 16, 18, 28, 40, 71, 72, 86, 95, 101, 106, 114, 116, 117, 119
Intrusion Detection System (IDS), 2–5, 15–17, 83, 86, 106, 113, 114, 116
Intrusion recognition, 3
Intrusive behavior, 5
Iris dataset, 16
Isomap, 9
Iterative minimization, 11

J
J48, 77
J − Rip, 77

K
K-means clustering algorithms, 10
Knowledge-base, 4
Knowledge Discovery in Data (KDD), 1, 5, 16, 17, 27–29, 39, 67, 72, 77, 83, 86, 94, 98, 99, 102, 113, 116, 119
Knowledge Discovery system, 15
K − Star, 77

L
Lazy IB1, 73, 74
Linear discriminant analysis, 9
Linearity, 9
Linear regression, 7
Linguistic labels, 18, 95–98, 106, 108, 116
Linguistic variables, 61, 96, 116
LMT, 77
Local, 11, 13, 15, 17, 79, 114, 115
Local discretization methods, 11
Logistic, 77
Lower approximation, 49, 50, 59
Lower triangle, 52

M
Machine learning, 11, 14–16, 34, 83, 113, 116, 119
Machine learning approaches, 3, 18, 114, 115
Machine learning based cut generation, 34
Mamdani model, 61, 62
Markov decision process, 83, 95
Mean absolute error, 39, 40, 73
Measured variable, 7
Membership, 10, 58–63, 66, 68
Membership function, 10

Merge the intervals, 12
Merging phase, 38
Minimal entropy heuristic, 13
Minimum description length principle, 13
Missing values, 6, 117
Misuse and anomaly detection, 4
Misuse detection, 4, 5
Modified-Q-learning, 114
Modified-Q-learning algorithm, 114
Modified_SAFC, 68, 70, 71, 77–79
Monograph, 113, 114, 116
Most Significant Cluster (MSC), 17, 48, 68, 71, 77, 78
Multidimensional scaling, 9
Multilayer Perceptron, 77
Multiple cuts, 13
Mutation, 65
Mutation procedure, 65

N
Naïve Bayes, 73, 74
Naïve Bayes classifier, 73, 74
Naive Bayes updateable, 77
Name of classifier, 73, 74
NB Tree, 73, 74, 77
Network-based, 3, 119
Network protocols, 1, 117
Network traffic, 15, 28, 116, 117
Network traffic data, 1, 16, 17, 27, 75, 113, 115
Neural networks, 3, 14
NNge, 77
Noise, 6, 7
Noisy, 15, 116
Nominal value, 27
Nonlinear, 9, 15
Nonlinearity, 9
Non-recurrent, 14
Non-stationary, 15
Normalization, 8
NP hard problem, 17
NR, 89
NSL KDD, 27, 83, 86, 94, 98, 102, 113, 116

O
Object reduction, 8, 10, 18
Optimal equal width interval, 17
Optimized Equal Width Interval, 16, 34, 40, 115
OR, 54, 90
Outliers, 6–8, 28

P

PART, 73, 74, 77
Particle Swarm Optimization (PSO), 34–37, 114
Partitional (k-means), 10
Password cracking, 1
Pattern evaluation, v
Patterns, 4–7, 15, 28, 47, 59, 61, 83, 113, 116
Pawlak, 113
Pearson's correlation coefficient, 101
Penalty, 14, 83
Personal best position, 35
Perturb_centre, 68
Polymorph, 4
Positive region, 49–51, 56, 57, 59
Potential attacker, 2
Precision, 42, 74, 75
Predefined threshold level, 12
Prediction accuracy, 8
Prevention of attacks, 3
Principal component analysis, 9
Probe, 5
Projection pursuit, 9
Protection of computer systems, 1
Protect privacy, 1
Pulmonary embolism, 76
Pulmonary embolism dataset, 16

Q

Q-functions, 83
Q-learning, 17, 18, 84–86, 95, 98, 106, 114, 116
Q-learning algorithm, 15, 18, 83, 86, 87, 95–98, 101, 104–106, 114, 116
Q-learning classifier, 15
Q matrix, 87, 88, 92, 94, 95, 101, 103

R

Random forest, 77
Random tree, 77
RBF Network, 77
Recall, 42, 74
Recurrent, 14
Reduct, 2, 10, 17, 18, 47, 51, 52, 54–58, 60, 63, 66, 76, 79, 86, 88–90, 96–99, 101, 104–109, 115, 116
Reduct formation, 55–57, 88, 116
Regression, 6, 7
Reinforcement, 14
Reinforcement learning, 14, 15, 18, 83, 95, 114, 116
Relative absolute error, 39, 40, 73

Remote to Local, 5
Remove inconsistencies, 37
Reward, 14, 15, 83, 85, 95, 96
Reward matrix, 18, 86–89, 92, 94, 97–99, 101–103, 105–108
Reward signal, 14
Ridor, 77
Root mean squared error, 40, 73
Root mean square error, 39
Root relative squared, 39
Root relative squared error, 39, 73
Rough set, 1, 2, 10, 17, 18, 47, 49, 50, 58, 59, 85, 115
Rough Set Theory (RST), 10, 16–18, 27, 47, 48, 51, 52, 55, 58, 59, 67, 68, 71, 79, 86, 88, 106, 113–116, 127
Rule-Base, 18, 60, 61, 98

S

Sampling, 6, 63
Sarsa, 15
Security attacks, 2
Security of resources, 3
Security policies, 1
Selection-based, 9
Self-organizing, 10
Semi Markov Decision Process (SMDP), 95, 96
Sequential Minimal Optimization (SMO), 77
Shannon's entropy measure, 13
Signature-based approach, 15
Significant cluster, 17, 48, 68, 71, 77, 78
Significant features, 8
Simulated Annealing (SA), 11, 17, 68, 114
Simulated Annealing Based Clustering Algorithm, 68
Simulated Annealing Fuzzy Clustering (SAFC), 17, 47, 67–69, 77–79, 115
Smoothing, 7
Snooping, 5
Soft clustering, 10
Soft clusters, 10
Sparse Matrix (SM), 92, 93
Split and Merge Interval, 16, 17, 34, 37, 40, 115
Split_center, 68
Split phase, 38
Spread, 16, 32, 33, 39, 40, 61, 115
Standard deviation, 28, 70, 96, 97
State action pairs, 83
States, 14, 18, 68, 83–86, 92, 95–99, 105, 106

State-space approach, 15
Static and dynamic, 1, 5, 11
Static classes, 5, 11, 13
Static methods, 5
Statistical approaches, 3
Storage devices, 8
Supervised, 11, 13, 14, 16, 34, 83
Supervised learning, 14, 34, 116
Supervised methods, 11
Support Vector Machine (SVM), 17, 47, 75, 79
Swarm, 34, 35
Swarm confidence, 35
Swarm intelligence techniques, 3

T
Temporal difference learning classifier, 15
Time-consuming, 7
Time-points, 7
Top-down, 11, 12
Training set, 34
Transformation, 6, 8, 9, 113, 117
Transformation-based, 9
Tree classifier, 73, 74
Tree data structure, 17
Trial and error, 14
Trial and error method, 14
Trial and error search, 14
True negative, 75
True positive, 42, 75

True positive rate, 74

U
Unauthorized user, 3
Unmanageable, 8
Unparameterized Supervised Discretization, 13
Unsupervised, 11, 14, 16, 34, 83
Unsupervised learning, 14, 34, 83, 116
Unsupervised methods, 11
Upper and lower approximation, 50
Upper approximation, 49, 50, 59
Upper triangle, 52
User to Root, 5

V
Vague data sets, 113
Value function, 83
Vulnerabilities, 1

W
Wine, 76, 77
Wine data set, 16, 96, 104
Wrapper approach, 9

Z
Zadeh, 113

Printed in the United States
By Bookmasters